IRISH BALLADS

IRISH BALLADS

CHARTWELL
BOOKS, INC

CREDITS

Editor
Fleur Robertson

Designer
Jill Coote

Production
Ruth Arthur
Sally Connelly
Neil Randles
Jonathan Tickner

Director of Production
Gerald Hughes

Text typesetting
Julie Smith
SX Composing Ltd, Essex

Music typesetting
Barnes Music
Engraving Ltd

Half title page
The Wicklow Mountains
courtesy of The Slide File

Title page
Mountain stream
courtesy of Don Sutton
International Photo
Library,
Folk musicians
courtesy of The Slide File

Facing page
Rosbeg, Co. Donegal
courtesy of The Slide File

CHARTWELL BOOKS
A division of Book Sales, Inc.
114 Northfield Avenue
Edison, N.J. 08837, USA

CLB 4650
© 1996 CLB Publishing,
Godalming, Surrey, U.K.
ISBN 0-7858-0633-4

Printed and bound in
Singapore

DEDICATION for Letitia Pollard

The publishers wish to express their appreciation of the assistance of Bord Fáilte-Irish Tourist Board's staff on the *Ireland of the Welcomes* magazine in the planning of this book. They acknowledge that the initial concept came from their special edition of the magazine *The Place in the Song: A musical Grand Tour of Ireland.*

CONTRIBUTORS

Diarmuid Breathnach (DB) is co-editor, with Máire ní Mhurchú, of *1882-1982 Beathaisnéis*, a biographical dictionary of the Irish.

Vincent Caprani (VC) is a freelance writer living in Dublin.

David Hammond (DH), film maker and broadcaster, is himself a singer of traditional songs.

Eoghan Ó hAnluain (EÓhA) is a lecturer at the Department of Irish in University College, Dublin, and chairman of Cumann Merriman.

Elizabeth Healy (EH) is a freelance writer and editor of *A Literary Tour of Ireland* and other publications.

Aoife Kerrigan (AK) is a tutor in St Patrick's College, Maynooth, Co. Kildare.

Benedict Kiely (BK) is a leading Irish writer; his auto-biography, *Drink to the Bird* was published in 1992.

Cormac MacConnell (CMcC) is a freelance journalist living in Galway. He comes from a well-known family of singers.

Ciarán Mac Mathúna (CMcM) is a well-known and much-loved broadcaster of Irish and traditional music. He produces and presents a very popular programme – *Mo Cheol Thú* – every Sunday morning on national radio.

John A. Murphy (JM) is Emeritus Professor of History at University College, Cork.

Nuala O'Connor (NOC) is a television producer and author of *Bringing It All Back Home.*

CONTENTS

❧ INTRODUCTION

These are the popular songs of Ireland, most of them over a century old and many as old, nearly, as the hills. They celebrate Irish people and places – the rolling hills, the deep glens, the jigsaws of islands on the broad loughs, the tidy towns, majestic rivers, star-high peaks and towering cliffs, sandy shores – all in dazzling variety, a kaleidoscope of rare beauty, physically and emotionally complex.

The songs have grown out of Irish soil as abundantly as wild flowers. They carry the hopes and fears, the joys and sorrows, the light hearts and ready smiles of the many fascinating cultures that have found a home in Ireland since early times. The melodies tug at the heart strings, echoing the subtle and changing moods of this varied island, the small intimate corners, dark shadows, glimpses of sunshine, the sudden gleam of yellow whin or a whitewashed gable in a clump of trees.

Their titles trip off the tongue like legends, mellifluous and evocative of the place and the spirit of the place, the *genius loci*. They are essentially Irish, well known and loved wherever Irish people gather, and yet not a few are known to a wider world. They live beyond their clan because the emotions within them are nothing if not universal in appeal.

BELOW: Brandon Bay at Cloghane on the Dingle Peninsula, Co. Kerry

Although these are some of the best-loved folksongs in the land, it was thought to provide the words of the songs and their music too 'so there would be no trailing off midway through the second verse'. Occasionally the songs appear in Gaelic, and then, where appropriate both the Gaelic and its translation appear. The people who wrote the texts for this collection have interests as diverse as the songs themselves – as novelists, historians, broadcasters, film-makers, journalists – and their texts reveal not only the factual backgrounds to the songs but also how close they are to the music and poetry integral to them. The history of a region, the life of a songwriter, the loves of a poet, the time-honoured events that grant a special place to a town, the legends that swathe a county – there is so much that can be revealed in the backgrounds to these ballads, and each writer's individual approach brings a slightly different twist to the glance back.

In times past these songs meant everything to our ancestors and they still mean much to us. They tell us and the world who we are.

David Hammond

ABOVE: sunlight on a tumbling stream in the Glens of Antrim

ABOVE: a ruined church window view of Donegal's Derryveagh Mountains

LEFT: 'You hum it and we'll play it!' Co. Clare musicians in Doolin

BY THE SHORT CUT TO THE ROSSES

The words of this song were written by Nora Hopper, set to an old Donegal air by Charlotte Milligan Fox and the song itself describes the unique atmosphere of the Donegal coastline in the north-west of Ireland.

Nora Hopper is an interesting writer, now hardly known, but in her own time recognised as a valuable presence in the Irish literary scene. She was born in Exeter in England in 1871 of an Irish father and a Welsh mother and, a prolific writer, she lived most of her life outside Ireland.

The Cabinet of Irish Literature said 'she makes up for her want of residence by saturating herself with Irish studies of all kinds: and few poets, hardly Mr. W. B. Yeats himself, have succeeded in becoming more thoroughly Irish'.

Later, when her own book *Ballad and Prose* was published around the turn of the century, the poet Yeats wrote about her work on the old Gaelic literature '… full of delicacy and charm … *Ballad and Prose* haunted me as few new books ever haunted me.'

Nora Hopper (she married a Mr. W. H. Chesson) died at an early age and this notice is included in *The Reciter's Treasury of Irish Verse and Prose* by Alfred P. Graves and Guy Pertwee, 'Her writings gave every promise that she would ultimately occupy a very high place in Irish literature and her untimely death was universally regretted …'.

The Rosses is that rocky land in west Donegal found between Gweedore in the north and Gweebarra in the south, a narrow coastal strip some twenty miles long and lying between the mountains and the sea. Here you are on the very edge of Europe with nothing before you but the wild Atlantic and nothing behind you but the towering slopes of Errigal and Muckish.

The Rosses comprise thousands of acres of craggy rock with small fields the size of your fist patterned by dry stone walls. When you look around you it is as if the bare bones of the earth are breaking through the entire landscape.

And always the light is changing as the Atlantic winds sweep over the land, bringing miraculous skies whose clouds form and reform, creating a vast bowl of brilliant light, a challenge for the artist and a benison for those who live there. A thousand lakes glint in the sun like mirrors and bog-brown streams tumble down to the sea, a halo of mist at every waterfall. There are vast stretches of sand, deep caves, arches, a necklace of islands from Arranmore to Owey Island and Gola to Inisfree.

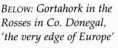

BELOW: Gortahork in the Rosses in Co. Donegal, 'the very edge of Europe'

The Rosses are so called from the Irish word meaning 'peninsula' and much of the district is still Irish-speaking. The beauty of the place is breathtaking but inhospitable and, although it is home for a huge and extremely dense population, in the scale of human history this seems to be a fairly recent development. There are ancient remains along this coast, but the population always remained small until the end of the eighteenth century. When Ireland's population radically increased in the 1700s there was not enough land to go around and families were forced westward in search of a living. There had been movement before that, of course, when political developments in East Donegal in the 1600s had displaced many families who had nowhere to go but west.

They could have chosen worse places than the beautiful Rosses.   *DH*

ABOVE: sunset at Bloody Foreland, from Ballyness Bay, near the Rosses

BELOW: tranquil Gweebarra Bay in the Rosses, Co. Donegal

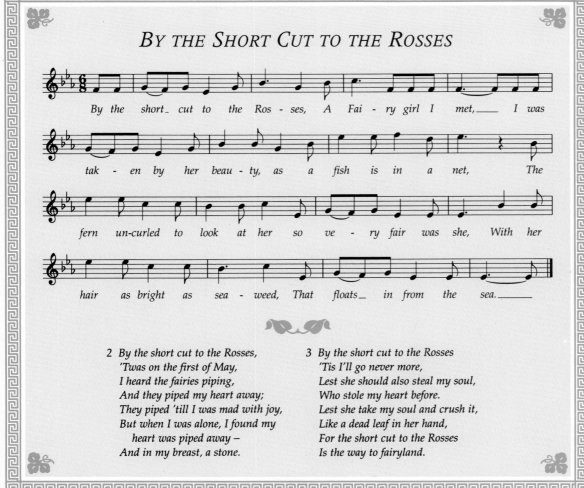

BY THE SHORT CUT TO THE ROSSES

By the short cut to the Ros-ses, A Fai-ry girl I met,___ I was tak-en by her beau-ty, as a fish is in a net, The fern un-curled to look at her so ve-ry fair was she, With her hair as bright as sea-weed, That floats___ in from the sea.___

2 *By the short cut to the Rosses,*
   'Twas on the first of May,
   I heard the fairies piping,
   And they piped my heart away;
   They piped 'till I was mad with joy,
   But when I was alone, I found my
      heart was piped away –
   And in my breast, a stone.

3 *By the short cut to the Rosses*
   'Tis I'll go never more,
   Lest she should also steal my soul,
   Who stole my heart before.
   Lest she take my soul and crush it,
   Like a dead leaf in her hand,
   For the short cut to the Rosses
   Is the way to fairyland.

THE OULD LAMMAS FAIR

This song was written by John H. Macauley, a carver of bog-oak and a native of Ballycastle, Co. Antrim. A plaque on the wall of his house in Ann Street in the town is a tribute to the memory of the man who made Ballycastle and its annual fair well known beyond Ireland.

The famous Lammas Fair in Ballycastle is unique, but it is just one of eighteen fairs that were once held during the year in the town. Like other small towns in Ireland, Ballycastle was a meeting-place for people from miles around. They arrived on set days to buy and sell and barter. Often the fair days coincided with a religious festival dating back to pagan times.

There are other famous fairs in Ireland still alive and doing well – the Horse Fair at Ballinasloe in Co. Galway and the Puck Fair at Killorglin in Co. Kerry, for instance. Many towns now only have the songs to recall the excitement of the day – like 'The Magherafelt May Fair' and 'The Hiring Fair at Hamiltonsbawn': most fairs have passed into history, their function superseded by phenomena like supermarkets and cars: people now travel further and more frequently in search of bargains and new experiences.

Ballycastle and its Ould Lammas Fair has survived and survived handsomely – it does not last a week now, as once it did, but on its single day it is still a great event for north Antrim people. If you are there you will be reminded that you are watching something which has been going on throughout the ages, when the country takes possession of the town, blocking its streets, ignoring its traffic. For the fairs were there long before the town started to grow up around them, associated with the celebration of occasions like seed-time and harvest, breaking the routine of toil and awakening a strong spirit of revelry when games and dancing (and even the occasional ritual row) were the order of the day once business was complete.

The atmosphere of the old fairs was robust, the bargaining competitive, as the dealers conducted the business with resounding slappings of open palms up and down the street; there were prolonged arguments, when curious onlookers gathered in a circle around the protagonists, about the amount of 'luck money'; horses stamped and shoved among the piles of goods spread out before the doors of shops, colliding with canvas-covered stalls.

It was a similar scene that John Macauley evoked in his song 'The Ould Lammas Fair'. In it a loving encounter between a man and a woman is enriched by his knowledge of the social fabric in north Antrim, authenticated with details such as personal names, place names and the delicacies of 'dulse and yellow man' ('dulse' is an edible seaweed harvested off the rocks at low tide and 'yellow man' a sticky confection of sugar and bread soda).

Ballycastle was well situated for a gathering, attracting country people from all over north Antrim, from the Glens of Antrim, from Rathlin Island and from nearby Scottish islands like Ailsa Craig and Islay. At any time you can see Scotland and the islands from the coast of Antrim: on a clear day you can spot sheep in the fields and the farmer amid his crop. The narrow seas between these lands have been a highway for travellers for thousands of years and the bonds of kinship and culture remain strong.

And the word Lammas itself? It's an Old English word for a harvest festival, literally a 'loaf mass'.

DH

ABOVE: 'dulse', a seaweed delicacy, at Ballycastle's Lammas Fair

RIGHT: 'Yellow Man', the sweet confection noted in 'The Ould Lammas Fair'

THE OULD LAMMAS FAIR

At the Ould Lam - mas Fair in Bal - ly - cas - tle long a - go, I met a lit - tle col - leen ___ who set my heart a - glow, She was smi - ling at her dad - dy buy - ing lambs from Pad - dy Roe, At the Ould Lam - mas Fair in Bal - ly - cas - tle oh, I ___ seen her home that night when the moon was shi - ning bright

Chorus

From the Ould Lam - mas Fair, in Bal - ly - cas - tle oh, At the Ould Lam - mas Fair boys were you ev - er there? At the Ould Lam - mas Fair in Bal - ly - cas - tle oh, Did you treat your Ma - ry - Ann to ___ dulse and yel - low man? At the Ould Lam - mas Fair in Bal - ly - cas - tle oh.

2 In Flanders fields afar, when resting from the war,
We drank 'Bon Sante' to the Flemish lassies, oh,
But the scene that haunts my memory is kissing Mary Anne,
Her pouting lips all sticky from eating 'yellow man',
As we crossed the silver Margey and walked along the strand
From the Ould Lammas Fair at Ballycastle, oh!

Chorus

3 There's a nate little cabin on the slopes of ould Knocklayd
It's lit by love and sunshine where the heather honey's made
By the bees ever humming, and our childers' joyous call
Resounds across the valley when the shadows fall,
I take my fiddle down and my Mary smiling there
Brings back a happy memory of the Ould Lammas Fair.

Chorus

15

SLIABH GEAL gCUA NA FÉILE
Bright and Hospitable Mountain

On the morning of the 26 June 1977, Cearbhaill O'Dalaigh, President of Ireland (retired), came home to Dublin all the way from China where he had been the guest of the government of the People's Republic. The same day that gentle scholar travelled to the little village of Tooraneena in Waterford to unveil a plaque to honour a local Gaelic poet Pádraig Ó Mileadha (1877-1947) on the occasion of the centenary of the poet's birth.

Pádraig Ó Mileadha (pronounced Mill-ay) came from this area, known generally as Sliabh gCua (pronounced Sleeve goo-a) which is part of the hilly countryside halfway between Clonmel and Dungarvan that is dominated by the Comeragh mountains to the north and east and the Knockmealdown mountains in the west.

Gaelic was the language of this part of the

FAR RIGHT: Dungarvan, where Pádraig Ó Mileadha once walked

BELOW: the Comeragh Mountains in the Sliabh gCua area of Co. Waterford

country when Pádraig Ó Mileadha was a boy. His grandfather Muiris did not speak English but he had a vast store of Gaelic songs and folklore, for indeed all this area of west Waterford had a long and rich Gaelic literary tradition, both oral and written, going back to the eighteenth century and before. Pádraig Ó Mileadha inherited this tradition and even in his teens started to write his own songs and poetry. His best known song is 'Sliabh Geal gCua na Féile'. This is how it came to be written.

In 1903, like many a young man before and after him, Pádraig Ó Mileadha took the emigrant ship, not westwards to America but eastwards to Wales. He settled in the little town of Clydach near Swansea and married a girl from his own part of Waterford and in time he became very involved in the trade union movement and in local politics. But over in Wales our poet's heart and mind were always back in the Comeragh mountains and in Sliabh gCua with the Gaelic ethos that still survived there. He thought of little places like Tooraneena (*Tuar an Fhiona mar a liontar an gloine* – the green pasture of the wine where the glasses are filled to the top). And so he poured out his feelings – the sadness of exile and the longing to be back – in this beautiful song 'Sliabh Geal gCua na Féile'. In fact Pádraig Ó Mileadha did go back in 1922 and spent the rest of his working life teaching and promoting the Irish language in his own countryside around Dungarvan.

Here we give an English translation of a song that is only ever sung in Irish.   *CMcM*

SLIABH GEAL gCUA NA FÉILE Bright and Hospitable Mountain

A Shliabh gheal gCua na féile, is fada uait i gcéin mé, Im shuí cois cuain i m'aonar, go tréithlag faoi bhrón. An tuile bhuí ar thaobh díom, idir mé agus tír mo chléibh-e Is a Shliabh gheal gCua na féi-le, nach géar é mo sceol Dá mbeinn-se i measc mo ghaolta i Scéithín ghlas na séimh-fhear Nuair a scaip-eann teas na gréin-e ó spéir gheal gan smál, Nó dá mbeinnse an-siúd faoin réal-ta nuair a thite-ann drúcht ar fhéar ann, ó a Shliabh gheal gCua nár dhéirc sin dá mb'fhéi-dir é a fháil?

1 'S é mo léan nach bhfuair mé tógáil le léann is mórchuid eolais,
I nGaeilge uasal cheolmhar ba sheolta mo bhéal,
Ó threabhfainn cuairt thar sáile is bhéarfainn bua thar barr chughat,
Mar, a Shliabh geal gCua, ba bhreá liom thú a ardú faoi réim.
Mo ghrása thall na Déise idir bhánta, ghleannta is shléibhte,
Ó shnámh mé anonn thar tréanmhuir táim céasta gan bhrí;
Ach ó b'áil le Dia mé a ghlaoch as, mo shlánsa siar go hÉirinn,
Agus slán le Sliabh na féile le saorghean ó mo chroí.

*Decie (pronounced Day-sha) is the Gaelic name for the general area of West Waterford.

1 O bright and hospitable Sliabh gCua,
I'm far away from you in exile,
Sitting alone by a harbour
Weakened with sorrow;
With the sea separating me,
From my beloved country,
Bright and hospitable Sliabh gCua
Isn't my plight just too painful?

2 If I were among my own people
In the green fields of Sceichin of the gentle folk,
When the heat of the sun spreads all over
From a cloudless sky;
Or if I were there under the stars when the
Dew falls on the grass,
O bright Sliabh gCua wouldn't that be a
Great charity for me if it were available.

3 All my love to the Decie* country, over there,
To its fields, its glens and mountains,
Since I sailed away across the sea I am weary
    and worn;
But if God wills to take me to Himself
I send my farewells westwards to Ireland,
And to the hospitable mountain,
With all my heart.

THE OULD PLAID SHAWL

ABOVE: Sir Thomas Alfred Jones' oil painting 'A Galway Girl'

BELOW RIGHT: The Ould Plaid Shawl pub in Kinvara, early morning

Francis A. Fahy, the author of 'The Ould Plaid Shawl', was born near Kinvara, Co. Galway, in 1854, but spent all his working life as a civil servant in London where he died in 1935. He was a founding member of the Irish Literary Society in London whose membership also included W. B. Yeats. When a branch of *Conradh na Gaeilge* (the Gaelic League) was formed in London in 1896, he became its first president.

As a writer, Fahy produced some very fine verse translations of Gaelic folksongs but he is best remembered for his own original song-lyrics in English, many of which were published in his *Irish Songs and Poems* in 1887. The musical arrangements were the work of such people as Alicia Adelaide Needham, C. Milligan Fox and Battison Haynes.

These songs became hugely popular and were sung at Irish concerts and gatherings all over England, America and of course Ireland itself. Now, a hundred years on, you can still hear a convivial company join in the chorus of 'The Queen of Connemara' or sing the praises of 'Little Mary Cassidy' and the little Irish *cáilín* in 'The Ould Plaid Shawl'.

P. S. O'Hegarty, a life-long friend of Fahy, described the songs thus:

> 'They are simple unaffected songs, songs of love and of home and of exile. They sing themselves, they demand to be sung, as do the songs of Moore and Lover and of Fahy's contemporaries, P. J. McCall and Alfred Perceval Graves.'

Colm O'Lochlainn, that great ballad collector, summed it all up as follows:

> 'His songs have cheered many in exile, brought tears to longing eyes and guided many a wanderer home.'

'I'll seek her all through Galway and I'll seek her all through Clare'. This was the journey our love-stricken hero of the song took on himself to catch up with the girl in the ould plaid shawl. Well, Kinvara is certainly an ideal starting point to explore Co. Clare and Co. Galway, even if your pursuits are not, as in the song, connected with affairs of the heart. As it happened, the poet Francis A. Fahy did find his own true love in Co. Clare, in Lisdoonvarna.

Kinvara is a charming seaside town on a sheltered harbour in the south-east of Galway Bay. Boats, old and new, have been part of its life since man first came there, way back in pre-history. Every year in August, Kinvara is host to a colourful festival called *Cruinniú na Bád* which

means 'the gathering of the boats'; and the harbour is full of sails and the taverns of the town itself full of traditional music.

Should you ever find yourself there, try to meet a local singer named Roisín Moylan, who sings the songs of Francis A. Fahy, particularly 'The Ould Plaid Shawl', accompanied by her father, Kieran Moylan.   *CMcM*

THE OULD PLAID SHAWL

Not far from old Kin-var-a, in the mer-ry month of May, when the
birds were sing-ing cheer-il-y there came a-cross my way, As
if from out the sky a-bove, an an-gel chanced to fall, A
lit-tle Ir-ish Col-leen in an ould plaid shawl, She
tripped a-long right joy-ous-ly A bas-ket on her arm, And
oh her face and oh her grace the soul of saint would charm, her
brown hair rip-pled o'er her brow but the great-est charm of all, was her
mod-est blue eyes beam-ing 'neath her ould plaid shawl.

2 I courteously saluted her, 'God save you, Miss', says I:
'God save you, kindly sir' said she, and shyly passed me by;
Off went my heart along with her, a captive in her thrall,
Imprisoned in the corner of her ould plaid shawl.

3 I'll seek her all through Galway and I'll seek her all through Clare;
I'll search for tale or tidings of my traveller everywhere,
For peace of mind I'll never find until my own I call
That little Irish colleen in her ould plaid shawl.

ABOVE: *Kinvara, a Galway Bay port, once home to Francis A. Fahy*

ABOVE: *'I'll seek her all through Galway and I'll seek her all through Clare ....'*

19

ARE YE RIGHT THERE, MICHAEL?

The Irishman was asked was there an Irish word for 'mañana'. 'There is, of course', he replied, 'but it hasn't the same sense of urgency'. This hoary joke carries a grain of truth. Even today the Irish countryman is not over-concerned with the clock. A century-and-a-half ago even the notion of standard time did not exist for the great majority. It was mainly the advent of the train which forced some form of synchronisation between the towns in that great network of railways that Ireland could boast at the turn of the century. The reasonable assumption that God had made plenty of time would not sit comfortably with the new regard for timetables. For those small lines struggling with an unfriendly terrain the challenge was often too great.

The entertainer Percy French used trains extensively to bring his one-man show to resorts along the western coast. One night in Kilkee, Co. Clare, he failed to turn up for a performance. It was the first and only time in his life. In fact his death at sixty-five is sometimes attributed to his insistence on giving a scheduled show. Even though he had a reputation for being happy-go-lucky, one can easily imagine the frustration he felt every time the West Clare stopped at a small halt such as Hanrahan's Bridge. There were seventeen such stops between Ennis and Kilrush. But the unscheduled stops, because of cattle on the line, for example, must have been

ABOVE: French's sketch of himself at a station: the guard says, 'The divil a train!'

FAR RIGHT: 'Slieve Callan' steam train, formerly of the West Clare Line

BELOW: sunset at Lahinch, where French claims 'the sea shines like a jewel'

nerve-racking for French, worrying about his audience in Kilkee. Some of the other obstacles in the path of the Wild West Clare he lists in the gentle revenge he exacted in this song.

In 1961, in line with the transport policy of the day, the West Clare railway was closed. It had lasted longer than almost all the other small lines. Something of the extent of the decline of rail since 1925 may be gauged from the fact that in the peak years there were approximately 1,400 railway stations. Today only one in twelve is left. Many of these stations were part of the romance of the discovery of remote places. The scholar Robin Flower claimed he could buy a ticket in Euston Station in London to the middle ages. He had in mind the Great Blasket, an island off the west coast which could be reached reasonably quickly from the rail terminus at Dingle.

Anyone looking at a railway atlas of Ireland for the year a 1912, say, is filled with nostalgia for a more easy-going age. 'Are Ye Right There, Michael', published in that same year, is now a part of that nostalgia.   DB

ARE YE RIGHT THERE, MICHAEL?

Ye may talk of Col-um-bus sail-ing a-cross the At-lan-tic-al sea, But he ne-ver tried to go rail-ing from En-nis as far as Kil-kee. You run for the train in the morn-in' The ex-cur-sion train start-ing at eight, You're there when the clock gives the warn-in', and there for an hour you will wait. And as you're wait-ing in the train, you'll hear the guard sing this re-frain: Are ye right there Mich-ael, are ye right? Do ye think that ye'll be there be-fore the night? Oh ye've been so long in start-in' that ye could-n't say for sar-tin, Still ye might now, Mich-ael, so ye might.

2 They find out where the engine's been hiding and it drags you to sweet Corofin
Says the guard, 'Back her down on the siding, there's the goods from Kilrush coming in.'
Perhaps it comes in two hours, perhaps it breaks down on the way;
'If it does', says the guard, 'be the powers, we're here for the rest of the day!'
And while you sit and curse your luck, the train backs down into a truck.

Chorus

Are ye right there, Michael? Are ye right?
Have ye got the parcel there for Missus White?
Oh ye haven't! Oh begorra! Say it's comin' down tomorra
And it might now Michael, so it might.

3 At Lahinch the sea shines like a jewel, with joy you are ready to shout,
When the stoker cries out, 'There's no fuel, and the fire is tay-totally out.
But hand up that bit of a log there, I'll soon have ye out of the fix;
There's a fine clamp of turf in the bog there; and the rest go a-gatherin' sticks'.
And while you're breaking bits off trees, you hear some wise remarks like these:

Chorus

Are ye right there, Michael? Are ye right?
Do ye think that ye can get the fire to light?
Oh, an hour you'll require, for the turf it might be drier
Well it might now, Michael, so it might!

THE SALLEY GARDENS

This lovely plaintive song was written by Ireland's most famous poet, W.B. Yeats, who was born in 1865 and died in 1939.

It was in Ballysodare village, Co. Sligo, that Yeats heard an old man singing the folk tune which inspired his version of 'The Salley Gardens'. Salley is from the Irish *saileach* or willow. Willow rods were used for basket-making and for providing scallops for thatching, and were grown specially for the purpose. There was once a row of small thatched cottages near the mills at Ballysodare (one of the mills had been owned by a great-uncle of the poet's), and each of them had a salley garden attached. There, by the river, was a perfect lovers' meeting place, as the song suggests.

ABOVE: 'Down by the Salley gardens ....' The Irish for willow is saileach.

THE SALLEY GARDENS

Down by the Salley gardens My love and I did meet, She passed the Salley gardens With little snow-white feet. She bid me take love easy, As the leaves grow on the tree, But I being young and foolish With her did not agree.

2 In a field by the river my love and I did stand,
And on my leaning shoulder she laid her snow-white hand.
She bid me take life easy, as the grass grows on the weirs;
But I was young and foolish, and now am full of tears.

Ballysodare is in the southern corner of County Sligo and acts as a kind of gateway to that county which, along with part of Leitrim, is spoken of as 'the Yeats Country'. The Unshin River flows through the town in a series of cascades. Ballysodare is *Baile Easa Dara* meaning 'The Place of the Cataract of the Oak' or, according to legend, the Cataract of Red Dara, a Fomorian druid slain by Lewy of the Long Hand.

When approaching the Yeats Country from the south, at Ballysodare one is already becoming conscious of entering an enchanted land. On the skyline far off to the left is Knocknarea, the hill on which Connacht's warrior Queen is buried under a huge burial cairn – 'where passionate Maeve is stony-still'; farther north is the great ship's prow of Ben Bulben mountain where the hero Diarmuid, lover of ill-fated Gráinne, was slain by an enchanted boar; and Lissadell, home of the Gore-Booth sisters ('both beautiful, one a gazelle') with its 'great windows open to the south'. One can tour the poetry, so to speak, around the lakes and under the strangely shaped hills, and even visit the Lake Isle of Innisfree and see if for you 'midnight's all a glimmer, and noon a purple glow, and evening's full of linnet's wings'.

Through his poetry, Yeats hoped 'to make every lake and mountain a man can see from his own door an excitement in his imagination'.

He was born in Dublin but there were strong family connections with Sligo, so that he spent much of his childhood in that region, and many holidays. Later in life he wrote: 'In a sense Sligo has always been my home'. His imagination was stirred by the stories he heard around cottage firesides – stories of fairies and enchantments, of gods and heroes and warriors. These legendary figures people his poetry, and have become inextricably linked with the landscape of the county.

Yeats is buried in the little graveyard at Drumcliff, 'Under Bare Ben Bulben's head'. *EH*

ABOVE: 'Bare Ben Bulben's Head' in Co. Sligo, near Yeats' grave

FAR LEFT: George Russell's 1897 portrait of the young poet W.B. Yeats

RAGLAN ROAD

Round about 1937 I first read of the poet Patrick Kavanagh who was to write, among many other matters, the moving love song that begins with that reference to Raglan Road in the south of Dublin City. What I read was an interview article in *The Irish Press*. It told how the interviewer went down to Inniskeen in County Monaghan to write about a young poet whose first collection, *A Ploughman, and other Poems* had just been published. And how the poet came striding to meet him across the poet's father's land reciting Yeats to the effect that he had been called an idler by the noisy set of undesirables, the martyrs called the world. Or something along those lines.

The interview article was signed by one Peter O'Curry.

Peter I next encountered in my first year at University College, Dublin, in 1940 or 1941. A paper on G. K. Chesterton, God bless us, I was reading to the English Literature Society and Peter was the visiting chairman. Afterwards he offered me a job on the weekly newspaper, *The Standard*, which he was then editing: and where

FAR RIGHT: a bronze of the poet Patrick Kavanagh, author of 'Raglan Road'

BELOW: 'On Raglan Road on an autumn day ....' Dublin leaves after rain

Patrick Kavanagh was later installed on a come-and-go basis. The friendship between the two men had endured and Kavanagh's collection *A Soul for Sale* was dedicated to Peter O'Curry and Anne, his first wife.

All that to explain why the first time 'Raglan Road' was ever sung was in the office of that weekly newspaper, then at the corner of Pearse Street and Tara Street in the heart of Dublin.

One day a college friend of mine, a student of law and history, called in to see me. Once upon a time in the Gaeltacht (Irish-speaking district) in Rann na Feirsde in Donegal, some sly joker had secretly taped that historian and myself trying to sing in unison an old Irish song. The result was Cacophony Beyond Description.

To the pair of us, then, as we sat talking in that newspaper office, came Patrick Kavanagh with a few sheets of paper in his hand. He slapped those sheets down on my desk. 'Could we sing that', he said, 'to the tune of "The Dawning of the Day?"' 'We could try', I said.

The John McCormack recording of the translation into English of *Fáinne Geal an Lae* ('The Dawning of the Day') was then most popular and I had even had the honour of meeting the great singer and notable gentleman. Not that that did anything for my own singing.

But the point was that the historian and myself knew the lovely lady referred to in the song. She was in college with us. And by showing us the song the poet was, most intimately, making his statement.

The three of us began to sing, or something, and went on until the door opened and Peter O'Curry burst in, saying: 'What, in God's name, is going on in here?'

And when we explained he gladly joined in to make up a quartet. Our hearts were in the right place. But our voices ….

That tale I once told to the late Luke Kelly of 'The Dubliners', who sang that song most movingly. And I feel that there was a tear in his gentle eye as he sang it again, there and then and just for me. *BK*

ABOVE: *Georgian Raglan Road, former haunt of Patrick Kavanagh*

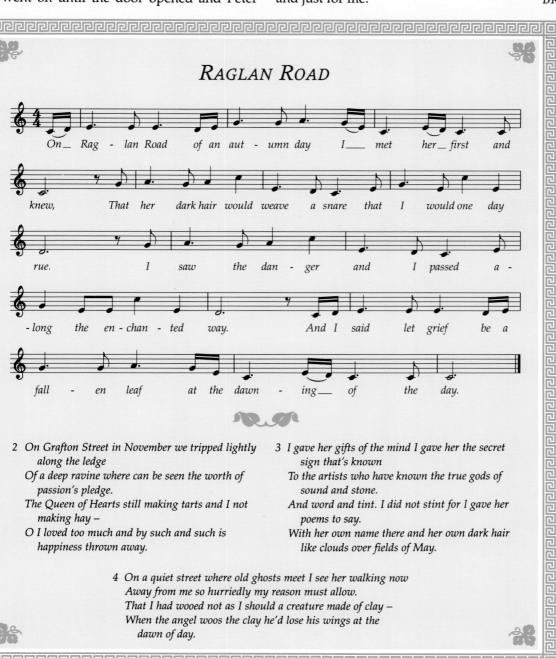

RAGLAN ROAD

On Rag - lan Road of an aut - umn day I met her first and knew, That her dark hair would weave a snare that I would one day rue. I saw the dan - ger and I passed a - long the en - chan - ted way. And I said let grief be a fall - en leaf at the dawn - ing of the day.

2 On Grafton Street in November we tripped lightly along the ledge
Of a deep ravine where can be seen the worth of passion's pledge.
The Queen of Hearts still making tarts and I not making hay –
O I loved too much and by such and such is happiness thrown away.

3 I gave her gifts of the mind I gave her the secret sign that's known
To the artists who have known the true gods of sound and stone.
And word and tint. I did not stint for I gave her poems to say.
With her own name there and her own dark hair like clouds over fields of May.

4 On a quiet street where old ghosts meet I see her walking now
Away from me so hurriedly my reason must allow.
That I had wooed not as I should a creature made of clay –
When the angel woos the clay he'd lose his wings at the dawn of day.

25

MY LAGAN LOVE

'My Lagan Love' is one of the most hauntingly beautiful of all the traditional Irish love songs, and it is not as widely known as it deserves. It can be classified among the *amhráin mór*, the 'high songs' of Ireland, and will not be easily forgotten by anyone who has been lucky enough to hear it sung well in the right atmosphere and circumstances. These seem to occur, it must be admitted, most often in the small hours when, according to one commentator, the nerve-endings are more sensitive but according to another, 'You just get more sentimental, that's all'.

Herbert Hughes was one of those indefatigable collectors of folk songs and airs without whom so many would have been lost for ever. He first heard this tune in 1903 played on a fiddle, and set about tracking it back as far as possible towards its source. He traced it back thirty years to a sapper of the Royal Engineers who had been working in Donegal with the Ordnance Survey of Ireland. The words were put to it by Joseph Campbell, who wrote the lyrics of several 'folk songs' including 'The Gartan Mother's Lullaby'.

The River Lagan flows through Belfast to the sea. Lagan Valley brings to mind the flax fields and mills for which it was famous – Belfast linen is still a family heirloom in many households.

ABOVE: Belfast Lough, where the River Lagan meets the sea, at sunset.

RIGHT: Sir Robert Ponsonby Staples' evocative work 'The Flax Pullers'

MY LAGAN LOVE

Where La - gan stream sings lul - la - by There blows___ a li - ly fair:

The twi - light___ gleam is in___ her eye, The night___ is on her hair.

And, like a love - sick len - an-shee,* She___ hath my heart___ in thrall;

No life I own, nor lib - er - ty, For Love___ is lord of all.

*fairy mistress, pronounced 'lanawn shee'

2 And sometimes when the beetle's call
Hath lull'ed the eve to sleep
I tip-toe to her sheeling low
And thru' her doreen peep.
There on a cricket's singing stone
She saves the bogwood fire
And hums in soft sweet undertones
The song of heart's desire.

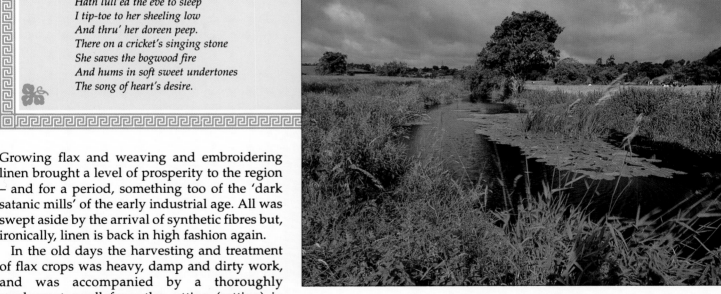

ABOVE: *the Lagan near its source, the likely setting for 'My Lagan Love'*

Growing flax and weaving and embroidering linen brought a level of prosperity to the region – and for a period, something too of the 'dark satanic mills' of the early industrial age. All was swept aside by the arrival of synthetic fibres but, ironically, linen is back in high fashion again.

In the old days the harvesting and treatment of flax crops was heavy, damp and dirty work, and was accompanied by a thoroughly unpleasant smell from the retting (rotting) in ponds of the flax cores, which then had to be spread to dry before the fibre was extracted. The woven lengths of cloth were later spread to bleach in the fields – a grand sight by all accounts, the long white ribbons contrasting brilliantly with the green of the meadows.

The setting for the song would seem likely to be high up near the Lagan's quiet source. The little stream emerges ten miles or so from Ballynahinch, above the village of Finnis which nestles under the knobbly head of Slieve Croob in an area of tumbled hills where the hand of man has been only lightly laid. In this old landscape a dolmen at Legananny has stood for 4,000 years or more, only slightly undignified by the necessary field fencing around it. *EH*

KILKELLY

Over one hundred and thirty years after his great-grandfather left the small village of Kilkelly in Co. Mayo, Peter Jones found a bundle of letters sent to his great-grandfather by his father in Ireland. The letters continued from 1860 until the old man's death in 1890. Though not exceptional in any way, they tell of family news, births, deaths, sales of land, and bad harvests. They also remind the son that he is still loved, missed and remembered by his family in Ireland. He, in the course of time, marries and has a family in America. One letter tells him that his brother who emigrated to England had returned and is thinking of buying land. The final letter, written by another brother, informs him that his father, whom he has not seen for thirty years, has died. And so the last tangible link with home is broken. Peter Jones used his great-great-grandfather's letters to make a song which he called 'Kilkelly'. The song was passed on to three Irish musicians living in the USA: Mick Moloney, Jimmy Keane, and Robbie O'Connell are professional musicians who make their living playing music with a strong traditional base. Mick, Jimmy and Robbie have made 'Kilkelly' their own. It has become emblematic of the kind of immigrant culture they try to bring out in their music. As far as Mick knows it's the only song written 'from the language of emigrant letters not just in the Irish culture in America but to the best of my knowledge, in any ethnic culture in this country'.

The song has had a deep effect on all audiences. It touches in some fundamental way on the spirit of the emigrant experience. Wherever it is sung people are moved to tears (as witnessed by this writer at a concert in Philadelphia). Mick describes 'Kilkelly' as 'the most eloquent and poignant tale of what it is like to be separated … the loneliness and the despair of it'.

NOC

KILKELLY

Kil - kel - ly Ire - land_ eigh - teen and six - ty, my dear and lov - ing son John,_____ Your

good friend and school mas - ter Pat Mc - Na - ma - ra so good as to write these words down._____ Your

broth - ers have all gone to find work in Eng - land, the house is all empty and sad,

The crop of pota - toes is sore - ly in - fect - ed a third to a half of them bad.

Your sis - ter Brid - get and Pat - rick O'Donn - ell they're going to be mar - ried in June,

Your mo - ther says not to work on the rail - road and be sure to come on home soon.

2 Kilkelly Ireland eighteen and seventy, my dear and loving son John,
   Hello to your missus and to your four children and may they grow healthy
      and strong.
   Michael has got in a wee bit of trouble I guess that he never will learn,
   Because of the dampness there's no work to speak of and now we have
      nothing to burn.
   Bridget is happy you named a child for her although she has six of her own,
   You say you found work but you don't say what kind or when you will be
      coming home.

3 Kilkelly Ireland eighteen and eighty, dear Michael and John my
      sons.
   I'm sorry to bring you the very sad news your dear old mother is
      gone.
   We buried her down at the Church in Kilkelly, your brothers and
      Bridget were there,
   You don't have to worry, she died very quickly, remember her in your
      prayers.
   And it's so good to hear that Michael's returning, with money he's sure
      to buy land.
   For the crop has been poor and the people are selling as fast as they can.

4 Kilkelly Ireland eighteen and ninety, my dear and loving son John
   I suppose that I must be close on eighty, it's thirty years since you've
      gone.
   Because of all the money you've sent me I'm still living out on my own,
   Michael has built himself a fine house and Bridget's daughters are
      grown.
   Thank you for sending your family pictures, they're lovely young
      women and men,
   You say that you might even come for a visit, what joy to see you again.

5 Kilkelly Ireland eighteen and ninety-two, my dear brother John,
   I'm sorry I didn't write sooner to tell you that father is gone.
   He was living with Bridget, she says he was happy and healthy down
      to the end,
   Ah you should have seen him play with the grandchildren of Pat
      McNamara your friend.
   And we buried him alongside of mother down at Kilkelly churchyard,
   He was a strong and a feisty old man, considering his life was so hard.
   And it's funny the way he kept talking about you, he called for you at
      the end,
   Oh why don't you think about coming to visit, what joy to see you again.

COCKLES AND MUSSELS

The popularity of a traditional ballad may be gauged by the types who sing it and by the frequency and the locations of its renditions. Dublin's anthem 'Cockles and Mussels' – like so many old songs from the pen of that ubiquitous and prolific poet 'Anon' – is 'known all over the world, and other places as well', in the words of an old woman in Moore Street. Indeed I myself claim the dubious distinction of having translated it into a kind of pidgin Italian for the famed Alpine male choristers of Coro Penna Nera and my Lombardian friends tell me that oft in the stilly night the groves around

FAR RIGHT: the statue of Molly Malone in Dublin's busy centre

BELOW: Walter Osborne's evocative painting 'St Patrick's Close, Dublin'

Samarate echo to the sonorous harmonies of 'A Dublino ci sono le fanciulle belle'.

And that bit of boasting is by way of saying that this is one of those airs more often sung by trained singers, choral groups, dance band vocalists and raucous football fans than by 'pure' ballad singers. That doyen of Dublin traditional singers, Frank Harte, says: 'Just because such a great song has fallen on hard times and mixed in the above company for too long, it should not be neglected by the unaccompanied singer'.

In a sense, too, the lady herself seems to have fallen on hard times. In recent years a researcher claiming to have located Molly Malone's death certificate in parish records mischievously suggested that her mortal fever was most likely a euphemism for venereal disease, thus hinting at activities other than wheeling a barrow. Those of us who gallantly dispute any imputation of promiscuity on our heroine's part would point to the more likely theory of her having contracted typhus from eating tainted seafood. We know that the development of Dublin port in the late eighteenth and early nineteenth centuries heralded the end of the once-flourishing oyster beds at Poolbeg, and contamination from domestic sewage forced the closure of similar beds at Clontarf, Sutton and Malahide, all in or near Dublin Bay.

Almost as little is known of Molly Malone's life as of the ballad's origin. Tradition has it that she lived in Fishamble Street and this is probably true. That narrow street owes its name to the medieval fish market, or 'shambles' (from the Anglo-Saxon *scamel*, a small bench) once

COCKLES AND MUSSELS

In Dub-lin's fair ci-ty, Where the girls are so pret-ty, I first set my eyes on sweet Mol-lie Ma-lone, as she wheeled her wheel bar-row, through streets broad and nar-row, Cry-ing cock-les and mus-sels a-live, a-live, oh!

Chorus

A-live, a-live, oh!___ A-live, a-live, oh!___ Cry-ing cock-les and mus-sels a-live, a-live, oh!

2 *She was a fishmonger,*
But sure 'twas no wonder,
For so were her father and mother before;
And they both wheeled their barrow,
Through streets broad and narrow,
Crying cockles and mussels, alive, alive, oh!

Chorus

3 *She died of a fever*
And no one could save her,
And that was the end of sweet Molly Malone,
But her ghost wheels her barrow
Through streets broad and narrow,
Crying cockles and mussels, alive, alive oh!

Chorus

ABOVE: *Temple Passage, Dublin – 'streets broad and narrow' remain still.*

ABOVE: *an eighteenth-century engraving of a typical street trader*

FAR LEFT: *Fishamble Street's sign. Here Molly is thought to have lived.*

held here. Be that as it may, Molly's statue at the junction of Grafton, Nassau and Suffolk streets seems set to become something akin to Rome's Trevi Fountain. Visitors to 'Dublin's Fair City' have started to toss coins into the cleft of her ample bosom and make a wish.

And Molly's song, which evokes her native place no less surely than the Ha'penny Bridge or the Custom House, will (in the words of the same woman in Moore Street) 'be sung forever, or even longer if required …'. *VC*

31

THE ENNISKILLING DRAGOON

RIGHT: Enniskillen's Royal Inniskilling Fusiliers Regimental Museum

BELOW: the interior of Blakes, a traditional pub for a song in Enniskillen

An island for every day in the year! Well that was what, as young people around Tyrone and Fermanagh, we always heard said about Lough Erne. Who counted the islands, or who vouched for the accuracy of the count, I never did hear.

One thing was certain, though: Boa Island which you crossed on the way from Omagh in Tyrone, through Fermanagh, and all the way to Bundoran in Donegal, was the greatest island of them all. A magic and beautiful place. You could even pause for a while when crossing that island to watch the young people at the crossroads' dances, or even to join them if you felt up to it. You envied the dancers and their lovely island and you envied the people of Enniskillen, Inniskilling, Enniskilling, because their magically named town belonged to that magnificent lake.

As for the Dragoons: their panoply and parading went away back to Wellington and Waterloo and more besides. It seemed fair enough that a romantic young lady from Monaghan town or thereabouts should fall in love with a young fellow all splendid in his crimson jacket. The words went well to the resounding pipe music.

In my own town we had a huge military barracks partially inhabited by gentlemen known as the Inniskilling Fusiliers. Not a horse between them. But the barracks then, and before these woeful times, were part of the town and a lot of my own boyhood was spent loitering around there admiring the spectacles, or playing football on the spacious sporting fields.

Perhaps a cynic might have said: 'a breeding ground for vocations for the British Army'.

My most moving memory of the pipes playing farewell on that great tune was when a collection of young fellows, some English, some Irish and school friends of my own marched off to France and Anzio and places further east: a good few of them never to return. *BK*

THE ENNISKILLING DRAGOON

A beau-ti-ful dam-sel of fame and re-nown. A gen-tle-man's daught-er near Mon-a-ghan town, as she rode by the bar-rack this won-der-ful maid, she stood up in her coach to see dra-goons on par-ade.

Chorus
Fare ye well Enniskillen, fare ye well for a while
And every blue border of Erin's green isle
When the war's all over we'll return in full bloom
And they'll all welcome home the Enniskilling Dragoon.

2 *These Dragoons were all dressed just like*
   gentlemen's sons
   With their bright shining bayonets and their
   carabine guns
   With their silver-mounted pistols, she observed
   them full soon
   For they were royal, loyal Enniskilling Dragoons.

   Chorus

3 *She looked on the brave sons of Mars on the right*
   With their armour outshining the stars of the
   night.
   Saying, 'Willie, dearest Willie, you have listed full
   soon
   To serve as a Royal Enniskilling Dragoon'.

   Chorus

4 *'Oh beautiful Flora, your pardon I crave*
   From this hour and forever I will be your slave
   Your parents they have slighted you both morning
   and noon
   All because that you love an Enniskilling
   Dragoon'.

   Chorus

5 *'Oh, Willie, dear Willie, don't mind what they say*
   For children must always their parents obey
   But when you leave old Ireland they'll all change
   their tune
   Saying, "The Lord be with the Enniskilling
   Dragoon"'.

   Chorus

ABOVE: *a nineteenth-century engraving of 'Sounding the Advance'*

BELOW: *an officer of the 6th Inniskilling Dragoons from an 1883 watercolour*

THE MEETING OF THE WATERS

One inevitably associates roses with Kilkenny: Rose Inn Street, the old Rose Hill Hotel, the Castle's rose garden, the county's anthem 'The Rose of Mooncoin' and that most famous of all roses which bloomed around 1810 in Jenkinstown, 'the last rose of summer'. It was a china rose (*Rosa chinensis*). A cutting from that same rose tree found its way to Dublin's Botanic Gardens and so the 'Thomas Moore' rose may be seen there to this very day.

The twenty-nine-year-old poet was one of the actors in Kilkenny's private theatre on The Parade, Kilkenny, in the season of 1808. Bessy Dyke was one of the actresses appearing with him in the following year. She was beautiful and

ABOVE: *The Meeting of the Waters in the Vale of Avoca, Co. Wicklow, today*

ABOVE: *the 'Thomas Moore' rose in Dublin's Botanic Gardens*

THE MEETING OF THE WATERS

There is not in this wide world a val-ley so sweet As that vale in whose bo-som the bright wa-ters meet Oh! the last rays of feel-ing and life must de-part Ere the bloom of that val-ley shall fade from my heart! Ere the bloom of that val-ley shall fade from my heart.

2 Yet it was not that Nature had shed o'er the scene
   Her purest of crystal and brightest of green;
   'Twas not her soft magic of streamlet or hill,
   Oh! no – it was something more exquisite still.

3 'Twas that friends, the beloved of my bosom, were near,
   Who made every dear scene of enchantment more dear,
   And who felt how the best charms of Nature improve,
   When we see them reflected from looks that we love.

4 Sweet vale of Avoca! how calm could I rest
   In thy bosom of shade, with the friends I love best,
   Where the storms that we feel in this cold world should cease,
   And our hearts, like thy waters, be mingled in peace.

under a certain tree and contemplated both the scene and his need of peace and the presence of his friends. The tree is now a stump, and the railway and the pyrite mines have not added to the glories of Avoca. The view of the Avonbeg joining the Avonmore from where Moore sat has, nevertheless, lost none of its charm.

Jenkinstown House, where Moore visited his friends the Bryans, is now mostly demolished, but 'The Last Rose of Summer' lives on as a great favourite with women singers. Even Beethoven himself made a setting of the air, and the German-born French composer, Friedrich von Flotow, incorporated it in his opera *Martha*. 'The Meeting of the Waters', on the other hand, retains its popularity among those of us with more limited vocal range, and for that reason it is presented here!   *DB*

FAR LEFT: 'Thomas Moore, Poet', a painting by Martin Shee (1769-1850)

BELOW: 'The Meeting of the Waters' by Thomas Creswick (1811-69)

only fourteen. In the play *Peeping Tom*, with Moore in the title role, she played Lady Godiva. Two years later they married and for the next forty years Bessy was the sole object of the affections of Moore, 'National Poet of Ireland' throughout the nineteenth century.

But his 'Last Rose of Summer' is not a love song. It is a song about love. The message is in the final verse:

> So soon may I follow,
> When friendships decay
> And from love's shining circle
> The gems drop away
> When true hearts lie wither'd,
> And fond ones are flown,
> Oh! Who would inhabit
> This bleak world alone?

Kilkenny was to hold a special place in the memories of Moore's courtship of Bessy. In June 1823 and again in August 1830 the theatre and club house (now a hotel), Jenkinstown and walking with Bessy along the Nore under the shadow of the Castle are recalled in his diaries.

The best of his Melodies – one hundred and fifty in all, published between 1808 and 1834 – were written before 1815. Among those best must be counted 'The Last Rose of Summer' and 'The Meeting of the Waters', the latter being written, it is usually said, in 1807, as the poet sat

THE GALWAY RACES

ABOVE: 'Strand Races' by Jack B. Yeats captures the spirit of fun at the races.

BELOW RIGHT: 'they never stood on ground': the Galway Races today

The Galway Races are held towards the end of July, but it was on 17 August that the ballad-maker's heart was elevated. He did not pick the date at random, for it was on that very day in 1869 that the Ballybrit course was opened. Lord St. Lawrence, the member of parliament for Galway, was the main drive behind the new venture. He had employed an expert, Thomas Waters, to lay out the course and design the stands. With special trains and a boat service from Cong across Lough Corrib, nothing had been left undone to make the day a success. The races of Galway were famous long before this, of course, and often not for the best reasons. Prince Pückler-Muskau, a great German traveller and friend of Goethe, was not impressed when he attended in 1828: 'Hundreds of drunken men accompanied our carriages as we drove down from the race course to the town'.

That great apostle of temperance, Theobald Mathew, had been active meanwhile and, leaving out the chorus in Irish which was borrowed from an older song, there is not a single word in the ballad about drink or dissension. The last verse, in fact, is exaggeratedly ecumenical. The presence of Jews and Presbyterians among the half million, even in small numbers, is unlikely. In the whole of Ireland there were no more than twenty Jewish families at the time. This and other exaggerations, such as those 'multitudes from Aran', lend charm and a feeling of conviviality to the descriptions.

Apart from one great verse there is nothing at all about the actual races in the song. At old style meetings, even within living memory, the sport of kings held little or no importance for many, when compared to *crúibíns* (boiled pig's feet) and other dainties, dancing, ballad singers, trick-of-the-loop men, fairground amusements, and the possibility, in the case of 'Clare unmarried maidens', of romantic encounters.

A little over a quarter of a century before this, another German traveller, Johann Georg Kohl, described an Irish race meeting. In the streets 'bagpipes were snuffling, violins squeaking, melancholy flutes blowing, and ragged Paddies dancing'. Ballad singers were as numerous as lamp posts. At the races dancing was going on in tents, there were shows and travelling theatres of all kinds, even a display of wild beasts and a puppet show. In 1842 William Makepeace Thackeray described similar scenes in his *Irish Sketch-book*. That same atmosphere, with every bit as much noise and clamour, but without the harrowing poverty, is captured in 'The Galway Races'. The stewards on the opening day at Ballybrit were Lords Clanmorris and Clanrickard, Valentine Blake and Henry S. Persse (of the same family as Lady Gregory). The sportsmen who travelled from Tipperary were probably also of the land-owning class. But the overall impression in the ballad, an impression created to some extent by the expressions of popular patriotic sentiment, is one of a homogeneous mass of common humanity, with everyone rubbing shoulders and being simply bent on enjoyment.   *DB*

THE GALWAY RACES

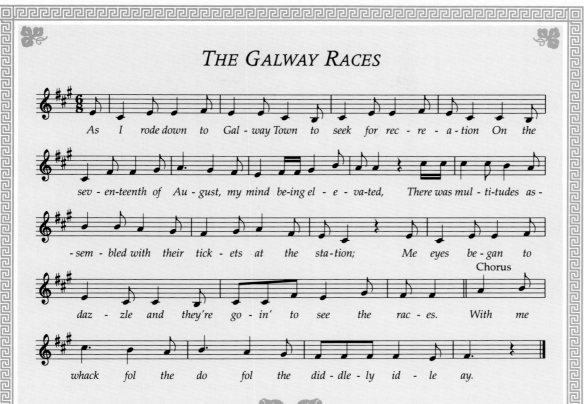

As I rode down to Galway Town to seek for rec-re-a-tion On the
sev-en-teenth of Au-gust, my mind be-ing el-e-va-ted, There was mul-ti-tudes as-
-sem-bled with their tick-ets at the sta-tion; Me eyes be-gan to

Chorus

daz-zle and they're go-in' to see the rac-es. With me
whack fol the do fol the did-dle-ly id-le ay.

ABOVE: 'nimble-footed dancers' enjoy Irish dancing in Co. Galway.

BELOW: the all-important winning post at the Galway Races

2 There were passengers from Limerick and more
   from Tipperary,
The boys from Connemara and the Clare
   unmarried maidens,
And people from Cork City who were loyal, true
   and faithful,
They brought home the Fenian prisoners from
   dying in foreign nations.

Chorus

3 It's there you'll see confectioners with sugarsticks
   and dainties,
And lozenges and oranges and lemonade and
   raisins.
And gingerbread and spices to accommodate the
   ladies,
And a big crubeen for thruppence to be pickin'
   while you're able.

Chorus

4 It's there you'll see the pipers and the fiddlers
   competing,
The nimble-footed dancers, and they trippin' on
   the daisies,
And others cryin' cigars and lights and bills for
   all the races,
With the colours of the jockeys and the price and
   horses' ages.

Chorus

5 It's there you'll see the jockeys, and they mounted
   on so stately,
The blue, the pink, the orange and green, the
   emblem of our nation.
When the bell was rung for starting, all the horses
   seemed impatient,
I thought they never stood on ground, their speed
   was so amazing.

Chorus

6 There was half a million people of all denominations,
The Catholic, the Protestant, the Jew and Presbyterian.
There was yet no animosity, no matter what persuasion.
But fortune and hospitality inducing fresh acquaintance.

Chorus

THE ROSE OF TRALEE

When the history of Irish popular song is written the *Nation* newspaper (1842-91) will have to be honoured with a full chapter. Its aim was 'to create and foster public opinion, and make it racy of the soil'. Songs were used to tell the estimated readership of 250,000 the story of Ireland in a racy manner. Contributing towards this purpose, in the company of such great songwriters as Thomas Davis, T. D. Sullivan and John Kells Ingram, was William Pembroke Mulchinock.

The Mulchinocks were people of some social standing in Tralee, Co. Kerry, but had come down a bit in the world, perhaps. In William's time they owned a drapery shop in the town and lived in Clogher's House near the River Lee, from which the town takes its name. *Tráigh Lí*, 'The clear crystal fountain' of the song, 'The Rose of Tralee', is nearby, although it is a long time since it deserved that description. Nearby also is the ruin of Ballymullan Castle. William must have heard the song:

Ballymullan old castle stands lonely and hoary
Silently glassing its shades in the Lee,
Telling in eloquent silence the story,
That hangs round its walls in the Vale of Tralee.

According to tradition, William fell deeply in love with Mary, the daughter of a woman who worked as a domestic servant for the Mulchinocks. Yet there were problems, both social and economic, that followed what was then known as 'marrying beneath your station', and so young William was quickly packed off to France. From there he made his way to India where he was wounded in a war. On arriving back in Tralee he saw a funeral coming down the street and was told that it was Mary's. He joined the cortege and, as soon as he reached home, wrote 'The Rose of Tralee', no doubt using the Ballymullan song as a model.

Having written poems for the *Nation* and other Irish journals, William left for New York in 1849, and gained a reputation there as a writer of lyrics. *The Ballads and Songs of W. P. Mulchinock* was published two years later. The list of patrons and subscribers include the poets Emerson, Longfellow and Whittier. 'The Rose of Tralee' is not in this collection. This omission was probably due to the fact that by this time William had married, or perhaps he considered it was merely an unsophisticated song, and not for the eyes of America's leading poets. He returned to Ireland in 1855 and died in Tralee at the young age of forty-five in 1864.

John McCormack's recording no doubt added to the international popularity of 'The Rose of Tralee'. At the turn of the century Irish

sentimentality was an essential ingredient even among lyricists who had never set foot in Ireland. Up to the 1930s it was among the most popular of the songs in the singing pubs of Lancashire.

Today Mulchinock's song has an international connotation of a different kind: the annual Rose of Tralee festival, the largest and most lasting of all the festivals which celebrate Irish eponymous beauties. It is highly probable that William Mulchinock would have preferred to be remembered by some of his more ambitious songs. But to have written the national anthem of his native county is no small achievement.   *DB*

THE ROSE OF TRALEE

The pale moon was ris-ing a-bove the green moun-tain, The sun was de-cli-ning be-neath the blue sea When I strayed with my love to the pure crys-tal foun-tain That stands in the beau-ti-ful vale of Tra-lee. She was love-ly and fair as the rose of the sum-mer, Yet 'twas not her beau-ty a-lone that won me. Oh, no! 'twas the truth in her eye ev-er dawn-ing That made me love Ma-ry, The Rose of Tra-lee.

2 *The cool shades of evening their mantle were spreading,*
And Mary all smiling was list'ning to me.
The moon thro' the valley her pale rays was shedding,
When I won the heart of the Rose of Tralee.
Though lovely and fair as the rose of summer,
Yet 'twas not her beauty alone that won me,
Oh, no! 'twas the truth in her eyes ever dawning,
That made me love Mary, the Rose of Tralee.

ABOVE: Ballymullan Castle, Tralee: 'lonely and hoary' still

ABOVE: a Rose of Tralee festival poster celebrates the annual August event.

39

Sweet Omagh Town

FAR RIGHT: *a cottage interior in Omagh's Ulster-American Folk Park*

BELOW RIGHT: *rich pasture around the town of Omagh, Co. Tyrone*

BELOW: *Bell's Bridge and the Sacred Heart Church at Omagh, Co. Tyrone*

The first complete singing that I ever heard of the fine song about Omagh Town came, oddly enough, from an Armagh man, a friend of that great Gaelic man of music, Sean O Baoighill. There was a collection of us on the way back from Rann na Feirsde in the Rosses, Donegal, and as a compliment to myself and a few others, and to honour the town we were approaching, in which I had grown up, that man of Armagh sang the praises of Omagh. We agreed with every word and joined in heartily.

Later on, in the course of a developing friendship with Paddy Tunney, that 'Man of Songs' from Lough Erne shore, I was to hear the song many a time and oft. And it was Paddy who, after considerable research, identified the author and composer: Michael Hurl from Annahonsh in the Newbridge area of South Derry, who lived most of his life in Luton and worked there as a journalist. What was it, I wonder, that set him singing not about Luton but about Omagh?

Omagh has a long history. The district was ruled by the O'Neill family for over a thousand years, from the fifth to the sixteenth century, passing to English rule after the flight of Hugh O'Neill, the second earl of Tyrone, in 1607. Today it is still clear why the O'Neills maintained so tenacious a grip on the place for so long: central and south Omagh is graced by fertile valleys, whose rivers are justifiably popular with anglers. Once pearls were collected from freshwater mussels there, salmon and trout teem still. Dairy cattle and sheep graze in rich pastureland, grouse shooting is still enjoyed. And to celebrate, each year the town is host to the West Tyrone Feis of Irish traditional

SWEET OMAGH TOWN

Ah from sweet Dun-gan-non to__ Bal-ly-sha-non, and from Cul-ly-han-na to

old Ar-boe, I've__ roved and ram-bled car-oused and gam-bled, where

songs did thun-der__ and whis-key flow, It's light and air-y, I've__

tramped thro' Der-ry, and to Port-a-fer-ry in the Coun-ty Down, But with

all my rak-ing and__ un-der-tak-ing, my heart was ach-ing for Sweet O-magh Town.

2 When life grew weary, aye, and I grew dreary
  I set sail for England from Derry Quay.
  And when I landed, sure 'twas fate commanded
  That I to London should make my way.
  Where many a gay night, from dark to daylight
  I spend with people of high renown
  But with all their splendour, and heaps to spend
      sure,
  My heart was empty for Sweet Omagh Town.

3 Then further going, my wild oats sowing
  To New York city I crossed the 'say'
  Where a congregation of rich relations
  Stood on the harbour to welcome me
  In grand apparel like Dukes or Earls
  They tried to raise me with sword and crown
  But with all their glamour and uproarious
      manner
  My lips would stammer of Sweet Omagh Town.

4 And when life is over and I shall hover
  Above the gates where Saint Peter stands
  And he shall call me for to install me
  Among the saints in that golden land
  And I shall answer, 'I'm sure 'tis grand, sir,
  For to play the harp and to wear the crown
  But I, being humble, sure I'll never grumble
  If heaven's as charming as Sweet Omagh Town'.

ABOVE: *a house front at the Ulster-American Folk Park near Omagh*

BELOW: *a nineteenth-century angler: Omagh's fishing was ever good.*

music, art and crafts. It an area to be proud of and the citizens of Omagh are indeed that.

For sure and for good reason, men from far and wide have praised my native place, and joined their voices with that of Frank McCrory, a notable Omagh man who wrote of:

'Dear Tyrone among the Bushes
You're the finest place I know.
To see again the winding Strule
A thousand miles I'd go,
And the rugged Glens of Gortin
And dear old Bessy bell ...'

BK

COME BACK PADDY REILLY

ABOVE: 'He'd dance the foot out o' yer boot'!

FAR RIGHT: four Paddy Reillys at the Percy French Hotel, Ballyjamesduff

BELOW: the many islets of Lough Sheelin, near Ballyjamesduff, Co. Cavan

Where is Ballyjamesduff? 'Just turn to the left at the Bridge of Finnea and stop when half-way to Cootehill': the directions in the song would not be at all helpful to the traveller.

Coming from Cavan town, turn left on to the Granard-Virginia road just before Finnea, and proceed along the shores of beautiful Lough Sheelin for nearly ten miles and you are there. The composer, William Percy French, would have known well 'the lie of it' but must have considered himself poetically licensed to drag in Cootehill. As an engineer, one of Percy's first jobs was on a Board of Works drainage scheme in County Cavan.

He spent seven years there, his duties bringing him around the country by bicycle or pony and trap. They were important years in his life. It was in Cavan he fell in love with Ettie, who was to be his first wife; he took up painting there; two of his greatest songs are set in the Cavan area – 'Phil the Fluter's Ball' and 'Come Back Paddy Reilly'.

O'Reilly is one of the dozen most common surnames in Ireland and in Percy's time the vast majority of O'Reillys were living in the Cavan district. Even today there are at least fifty 'Paddy Reillys' in the telephone directory for the

area. In Percy's time in Cavan the 'O' (which means grandson or descendant) and the 'Mac' had been dropped by many, but today it has been resumed by at least three-quarters of the ancient O'Reilly sept.

There is an O'Reilly castle on an islet off the shores of nearby Lough Sheelin. It was on the Bridge of Finnea on 5 August 1646 that the legendary Myles the Slasher O'Reilly performed his Horatius-like feats:

> He fought till the dead and the dying
> Heaped high on the battlements lay;
> He fell, but the foot of the foeman
> Passed not o'er the Bridge of Finnea.

Why did Percy choose Ballyjamesduff? A challenge to feature the town in a song has been suggested as a reason. Whatever the truth, it would be fair to say that French, whose background was somewhat upper crust, had an ear for the comic effect of some Irish place-names. The incongruity of Ballyjamesduff as the Garden of Eden would be bound to raise a smile. The best known, perhaps, of his great songs, 'Come Back Paddy Reilly' certainly placed the small town squarely on the map.   DB

Come Back Paddy Reilly

The Gar-den of E-den has van-ished they say, But I know the lie of it still._____ Just turn to the left at the bridge of Fin-ea, And stop when half way to Coote Hill._____ 'Tis there I will find it I know sure e-nough. When for-tune has come to my call._____ Oh, the grass it is green a-round Bal-ly-james-duff And the blue sky is o-ver it all!_____ And tones that are ten-der, and tones that are gruff Are whis-per-ing o-ver the sea:_____ 'Come back Pad-dy Reil-ly to Bal-ly-james-duff. Come home Pad-dy Reil-ly to me.'_____

2 My mother once told me that when I was born.
The day that I first saw the light.
I looked down the street on that very first morn
And gave a great crow of delight.
Now most new-born babies appear in a huff
And start with a sorrowful squall,
But I know I was born in Ballyjamesduff
And that's why I smile on them all!
The baby's a man now, he's toil-worn and tough.
Still, whispers come over the sea.
'Come back, Paddy Reilly, to Ballyjamesduff
Come home, Paddy Reilly, to me'.

3 The night that we danced by the light o' the moon.
Wid Phil to the fore wid his flute.
When Phil threw his lip over 'Come again soon',
He'd dance the foot out o' yer boot.
The day that I took long Magee by the scruff,
For slanderin' Rosie Kilrain;
Then marchin' him straight out of Ballyjamesduff,
Assisted him unto a drain.
Oh, sweet are me dreams as the dudeen I puff,
Of whisperings over the sea.
'Come back, Paddy Reilly, to Ballyjamesduff
Come home, Paddy Reilly, to me'.

4 I've loved the young women of every land,
That always came easy to me.
Just barrin' the belles of the Blackamore brand,
And chocolate shapes of Feegee,
But that sort of stuff is a moon-shining stuff,
And never will addle me brain;
For bells will be ringin' in Ballyjamesduff
For me and me Rosie Kilrain.
And all through their glamour, their gas and their guff,
A whisper comes over the sea,
'Come back, Paddy Reilly, to Ballyjamesduff,
Come home, Paddy Reilly, to me'.

THE LONDONDERRY AIR

Derry is located in the north-west corner of Northern Ireland, close to Donegal and at the head of Lough Foyle. The lovely hilly old city is full of atmosphere and the signposts of history. It's also full of loquacious, witty people who love telling strangers about their city, especially about that famous event, the Siege of Derry, as if it were a battle just lost or won, rather than something that happened three hundred years before.

The core of Derry is a completely walled town on the steep slopes of a hill that was originally an island in the River Foyle. It still retains its medieval layout of a central 'diamond' with four main streets radiating to the original four gateways in the walls. The city presses close up against the walls; in fact the walls are part of the normal day-to-day pedestrian thoroughfare. They are also the best viewpoint for the city. About a mile around and still intact, they were built by a group of London merchants who were granted the town in 1609. It was at that stage that 'London' was added to the name; both name-styles have their advocates nowadays.

BELOW: King James II of England, who failed to break the Siege of Derry

BELOW: the Apprentice Boys close the gates in Derry's Guildhall glass.

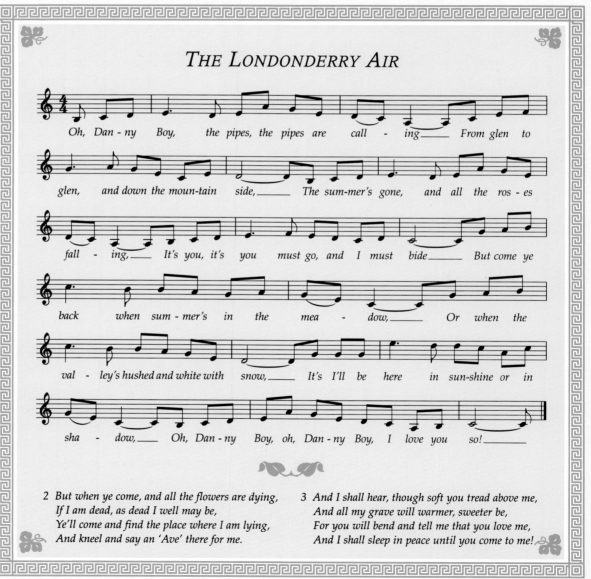

THE LONDONDERRY AIR

Oh, Danny Boy, the pipes, the pipes are calling From glen to glen, and down the mountainside, The summer's gone, and all the roses falling, It's you, it's you must go, and I must bide But come ye back when summer's in the meadow, Or when the valley's hushed and white with snow, It's I'll be here in sunshine or in shadow, Oh, Danny Boy, oh, Danny Boy, I love you so!

2 But when ye come, and all the flowers are dying,
If I am dead, as dead I well may be,
Ye'll come and find the place where I am lying,
And kneel and say an 'Ave' there for me.

3 And I shall hear, though soft you tread above me,
And all my grave will warmer, sweeter be,
For you will bend and tell me that you love me,
And I shall sleep in peace until you come to me!

But to get back to the famous siege. It is ironic that so dramatic a happening, one which continues to affect our lives down to this day, had little or nothing to do with Ireland as far as the main participants were concerned. It was part of a war between two kings for the throne of England, fought out almost by accident on Irish soil.

When William of Orange made a bid for the throne of England, he was welcomed with open arms by the English who were suspicious of the lawful King James II, he being a devout Catholic convert. James fled to France and then to Ireland to rally support. Ireland rallied behind him – all but Protestant Derry. When a new detachment of troops loyal to James set out to replace the old city garrison, the citizens of Derry became convinced they were all going to be massacred. While the elders dithered, a group of apprentice boys slammed the gates against the new garrison. The die was cast, and a siege began which was to last a hundred and five agonising days: in the end a rat, for anyone lucky enough to be able to get one, cost one shilling (a large sum in those days), a mouse sixpence. The arrival of King James himself before the gates only made matters worse: a cannon was fired at him, an extraordinary act of defiance against the legitimate monarch. There was 'No Surrender' and finally aid came to the besieged city via a ship that broke the boom. James and his army marched away, to later and further defeat at the Boyne by William himself, who had pursued James to Ireland.

The War of the Kings dragged on for two years but the happenings at Derry played a significant part in the final defeat of King James and in the course of Irish history in the centuries since.

The dramatic happenings of those years are depicted in the Guildhall in Derry in a truly astonishing array of stained glass.

That's the story of Derry. Such stirring deeds bear little relation to the quiet surrounding county. It was at Limavady to the north-east that one Jane Ross heard and recorded the air, and it was published as a tune without title in 1855. There have been several lyrics attached to it since. John MacCormack sang it as 'Mary Dear', and an Irish version gives *Maidin i mBéara* –'Morning in Beara'– which is in the extreme south-west, about as far from Derry as one could get in Ireland. The version which has become most popular – often known as 'Danny Boy' – was written by Fred Weatherley, an English barrister who was a fine opera librettist.

Sir Hubert Parry pronounced 'The Londonderry Air' 'the most beautiful folk tune in the world'. It certainly is one of the noblest song airs to come out of Ireland.   *EH*

ABOVE: 'But come ye back when summer's in the meadow ....' Limavady

BELOW: strong and steadfast Derry city walls still stand tall today.

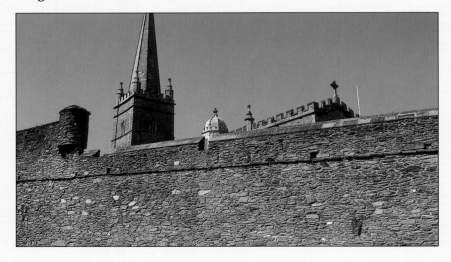

BANTRY BAY & THE KERRY DANCES

James Lynam Molloy wrote many songs, but the three best-known ones are 'Bantry Bay','The Kerry Dance' and 'Love's Old Sweet Song' ('Just a Song at Twilight'). We are concerned here with the first two (see overleaf).

In 'Bantry Bay' the girls are waiting on the pier with their baskets for the fishermen to come home. Here in West Cork, as in the fishing village of Claddagh in Galway and in many other such villages in Ireland and, indeed, all over maritime Europe, the women took charge of the fish once they were landed and bought them for sale in baskets very often carried on their heads.

'Bantry Bay' and 'The Kerry Dance', like many

FAR RIGHT: 'Lads and lassies to your places ....' Irish dancing today

RIGHT: folk musicians playing the uilleann pipes and the bodhran

BELOW: 'In the gloaming the shadows of the past draw near ....' Bantry Bay

other Irish songs, are full of nostalgia, full of memories of youthful days, memories of boys and girls dancing in the open air to the music of a piper.

Now when James Lynam Molloy was a young man, in the middle of the nineteenth century, the piper was a familiar figure in rural Ireland. (These Irish pipes are a much more sophisticated instrument than the Scottish war-pipes and are blown, not from a mouthpiece, but by a bellows under one arm.) Molloy obviously knew this music tradition well and introduces a piper into these songs:

> O the days of the Kerry dancing
> O the ring of the piper's tune
> O for one of those hours of gladness
> Gone, alas, like our youth too soon.
>
> The Kerry Dances

> Then we heard the piper's sweet note tuning,
> And all the lassies turn'd to hear:
> As they mingled with a soft voice crooning,
> Till the music floated down the wooden pier.
>
> Bantry Bay

James Lynam Molloy did not belong to the Cork-Kerry traditional community which he loved to write about. He was born in Offaly in the Midlands in 1837, the son of a local doctor, and was educated at the Catholic University in Dublin, at London University and also in Paris and Bonn. In 1872 he was called to the Bar at the Middle Temple in London. The law, however, had no attraction for him and he never practised; he was far more interested in becoming a songwriter, which indeed he did.

Molloy's songs are still great favourites but they do need a good voice even at informal gatherings where decent people meet to sing and to clink a glass or two. And speaking of favourites we must mention another of Molloy's songs which went all over the world and for which he gets little credit – 'Love's Old Sweet Song', also known as 'Just a Song at Twilight'.

If the composer of 'Bantry Bay' and 'The Kerry Dance' were to come back today he would be pleased to find that the music of the piper and the fiddler and the flute and the concertina is very much alive, while the country dances have become fashionable again all over Ireland, with young and old alike. Still 'a tender sound of song and merry dancing' steals 'softly over Bantry Bay'. *CMcM*

ABOVE: Irish fisher girls at work on a quayside at the turn of the century

LEFT: 'In the glen of a summer's night ....' Killarney, Co. Kerry

BANTRY BAY

1. As I'm sit-ting all a-lone in the gloam - ing, It might have been but yes - ter -
2. Then we heard the pip-er's sweet note___ tun - ing, And all the lass-ies turned to

- day, That we watched the fish-er sails all___ hom - ing, til the
hear, As they min-gled with a soft voice___ croon - ing, til the

lit - tle her-ring fleet at an-chor lay, Then the fish-er girls with bas-kets___
mu - sic float-ed down the wood-en pier, 'Save you kind-ly Col-leens all!' said the

swing - ing, came run-ning down the old stone way, Ev - 'ry
pip - er, 'Hands a-cross and trip it while I play,' And a

las - sie to her sail-or lad was sing - ing, A wel-come back to Ban-try Bay. 3. As I'm
ten - der sound of song and mer-ry danc - ing! Stole soft-ly o - ver Ban-try Bay.

sit - ting all a-lone in the gloam - ing the sha-dows of the past draw near, And I

see the lov-ing fa-ces___ round me, That used to glad the old brown pier, Some are

Rall.

gone up-on their last lov'd___ hom - ing Some are left but they are old and grey And we're

wait-ing for the tide in the gloam - ing To sail up-on the great high-way. To the

land___ of___ rest___ un - end - ing All peace-ful-ly from Ban-try Bay.

THE KERRY DANCE

1. O the days of the Ker - ry Dan - ces, O the ring of the Pip - er's tune, O for one of those hours of glad - ness,
2. Was there ev - er a sweet - er col - leen, In the dance than Ei - ly More, Or a proud - er lad than Thad - y,

Gone, a - las like our youth too soon, When the boys be - gan to gath - er, In the glen of a sum - mer night,
As he bold - ly took the floor, Lads and lass - ies to your plac - es, Up the mid - dle and down a - gain,

And the Ker - ry pip - er's tun - ing made us long_ with wild de - light, O to think of it, O to dream of it,
And the mer - ry heart - ed laugh - ter ris - ing through the hap - py glen.

fills my heart with tears, O the days of the Ker - ry Dan - ces, O the ring of the Pip - er's tune,

O for one of those hours of glad - ness, Gone, a - las like our youth too soon. 3. Time goes on____ and the

hap - py years are dead__ And one by one___ the mer - ry hearts are fled,___ Si - lent now___ is the

wild and lone - ly glen,___ Where the bright glad laugh__ will e - cho ne'er a - gain. On - ly dream - ing of

Rall.

days gone by, In my heart I hear. Lov - ing voi - ces of old com - pan - ions, steal - ing out of the

past once more, And the sound of the dear old mu - sic, soft and sweet as in days of yore, When the boys be -

- gan to gath - er in the glen of a sum - mer's night, and the Ker - ry pip - er's tun - ing, made us long_ with

wild de - light, O to think of it, O to dream of it fills my heart with tears. O the days of the Ker - ry dan - ces,

O the ring of the pip - er's tune, O for one of those hours of glad - ness, Gone a - las like our youth too soon.

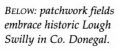

GLEN SWILLY

This song is included both in honour of a dear lady, Nora Harkin, née MacGinley, and in honour of the beauty of the remote glen that it celebrates. Nora, at eighty-five years young, is the most warmhearted, hospitable and lovely woman one could meet walking all the roads of the world. She has the wild and wonderful turn of phrase of her region, a great sense of the absurd, and her funniest stories are told against herself. For all that, she has been a serious and effective campaigner on political and social issues all her life.

It was Nora's father, Michael MacGinley, who wrote the words of this song as a young man on board the *Inver Cargill*, a sailing ship bound for Australia, a journey of ninety-one days. He was driven not by hunger but by the lure of adventure, and when he felt he had seen enough, he returned home to Donegal and opened a pub in the town of Letterkenny.

Glen Swilly is a sparsely populated valley opening into the hills from Lough Swilly, a great sea-arm probing deep into County Donegal from the North Atlantic, at almost the most northerly point of Ireland. On one side lies the tumbled land of the Inishowen Peninsula, on the other the great headlands of Fanad and Rosguill, lands of heart-stopping loveliness, sand and cliff and rock and sea-breakers. To the west the Derryveagh Mountains carve a jagged skyline, cradling the exquisite lake, castle and gardens of Glenveagh National Park.

When Nora MacGinley was a young girl growing up in this mountainy world, times were hard and people were poor. But they had music and story-telling, neither of which required riches. As she talks about stories around the winter fireside, and dancing at the crossroads on summer evenings, she'll say, 'Ah, but we were so light-hearted'.

Lough Swilly figures largely over a long stretch of Irish history. It was from here that young chief Red Hugh O'Donnell was snatched aboard a ship and taken to Dublin Castle in 1587, to escape four years later and cross the frozen wilderness of the Wicklow mountains on Christmas night in a blizzard. From here also took place that tragic exodus which came to be known as 'The Flight of the Earls', when the chieftain of the north, 'the Great O'Neill' and others, defeated at last, took ship for the Continent in 1607, never to return.   *EH*

BELOW: patchwork fields embrace historic Lough Swilly in Co. Donegal.

GLEN SWILLY

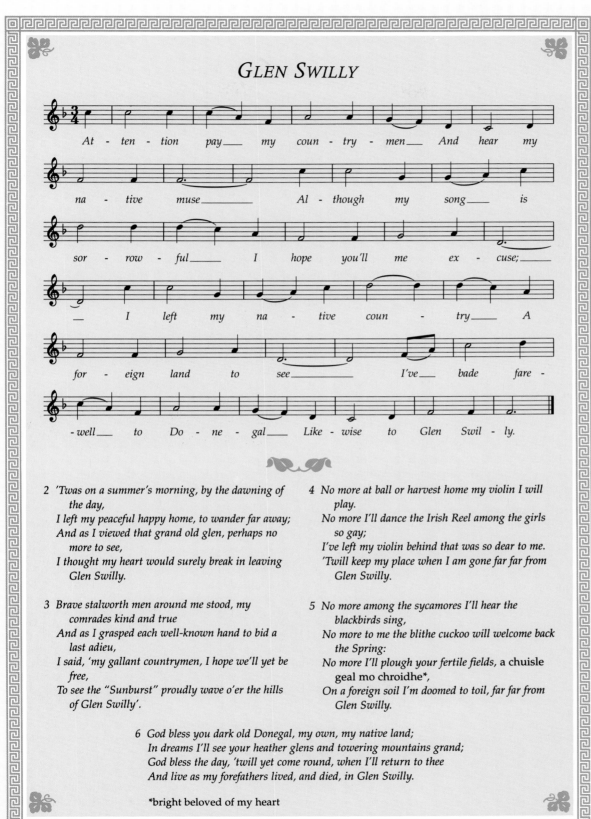

At - ten - tion pay__ my coun - try - men__ And hear my
na - tive muse_____ Al - though my song__ is
sor - row - ful____ I hope you'll me ex - cuse;___
__ I left my na - tive coun - try___ A
for - eign land to see_____ I've__ bade fare -
- well__ to Do - ne - gal__ Like - wise to Glen Swil - ly.

ABOVE: Nora Harkin surveying her father's beloved Glen Swilly.

BELOW: Glen Swilly's pastures and stream where sheep are grazed today

2 'Twas on a summer's morning, by the dawning of
  the day,
  I left my peaceful happy home, to wander far away;
  And as I viewed that grand old glen, perhaps no
  more to see,
  I thought my heart would surely break in leaving
  Glen Swilly.

3 Brave stalworth men around me stood, my
  comrades kind and true
  And as I grasped each well-known hand to bid a
  last adieu,
  I said, 'my gallant countrymen, I hope we'll yet be
  free,
  To see the "Sunburst" proudly wave o'er the hills
  of Glen Swilly'.

4 No more at ball or harvest home my violin I will
  play.
  No more I'll dance the Irish Reel among the girls
  so gay;
  I've left my violin behind that was so dear to me.
  'Twill keep my place when I am gone far far from
  Glen Swilly.

5 No more among the sycamores I'll hear the
  blackbirds sing,
  No more to me the blithe cuckoo will welcome back
  the Spring:
  No more I'll plough your fertile fields, a chuisle
  geal mo chroidhe*,
  On a foreign soil I'm doomed to toil, far far from
  Glen Swilly.

6 God bless you dark old Donegal, my own, my native land;
  In dreams I'll see your heather glens and towering mountains grand;
  God bless the day, 'twill yet come round, when I'll return to thee
  And live as my forefathers lived, and died, in Glen Swilly.

*bright beloved of my heart

WHERE THE SHANNON RIVER MEETS THE SEA

In this song two sentiments combine and fuse, the love of a place and the love for a beautiful girl who lives there and 'whose blue eyes mean all the world' to the poet who, alas! is far away.

The Shannon, Ireland's longest river, follows its course from its source in Cavan down through the centre of the country to Limerick, where it makes a sharp right turn and goes the last fifty miles to join the sea between Clare on the north bank and Kerry on the south. Yet the marriage of the two begins well up the estuary, for the sea as groom travels up to meet his Shannon bride and, in fact, the river is tidal as far up as Limerick City. But the real mouth of the Shannon is measured between Kerry Head on the south side and Loop Head in Clare. According to tradition, Cúchulainn, the legendary warrior of Irish mythology, once jumped from the Kerry side to Loop Head (it's only ten miles across) thus giving the name to the Clare promontory, *Ceann Láme* (meaning the headland of the leap), later anglicised to Loop Head.

The Shannon estuary is full of history. In the eighth century the Vikings sailed in and settled in Limerick, but their supremacy was ended by King Brian Boru, the Clareman, in 1014.

FAR RIGHT: Shannon Pot, Co. Cavan, the source of Ireland's longest river

BELOW: Virgin Rock at Ballybunion, at the mouth of the River Shannon

In the twelfth century the Normans arrived and settled along the Shannon and their descendants are still there, with many of them becoming more Irish than the Irish themselves. One such family is the Fitzgeralds, the Knights of Glin, who still occupy Glin Castle right on the banks of the Shannon about thirty miles down the estuary from Limerick city.

The countryside on both sides of the mouth of the Shannon is spectacular in its landscape and seascape. On the Clare side you have fine cliff scenery and also the very popular seaside resort of Kilkee. The resort of Ballybunion on the Kerry side has one of the most famous golf links in the world, a favourite of the great American golfer Tom Watson.

'Clare for music and Kerry for writers'. True enough, Clare has a widespread reputation for its traditional music festivals and Kerry has many famous writers. Bryan MacMahon, John B. Keane, Brendan Kennelly, and the Writers' Week in Listowel in May attract lovers of literature from many lands.

If you wish to travel from Kerry to the coast of

West Clare or from Clare to Kerry you won't have to leap these days as Cúchulainn was obliged to do. The car ferry from Tarbert on the Kerry side to Killimer in Clare will get you there in twenty minutes and it runs all the year round during daylight hours.

On the way across the Shannon you can sing this song and hope that the poor lover whose feet were 'planted in a far-off land' did eventually get back to his blue-eyed girl 'Where the Shannon River Meets the Sea'.   *CMcM*

ABOVE: *the cliffs of Loop Head peninsula near Kilkee in Co. Clare*

ABOVE: *'Returning to my darling ....' A nineteenth-century engraving*

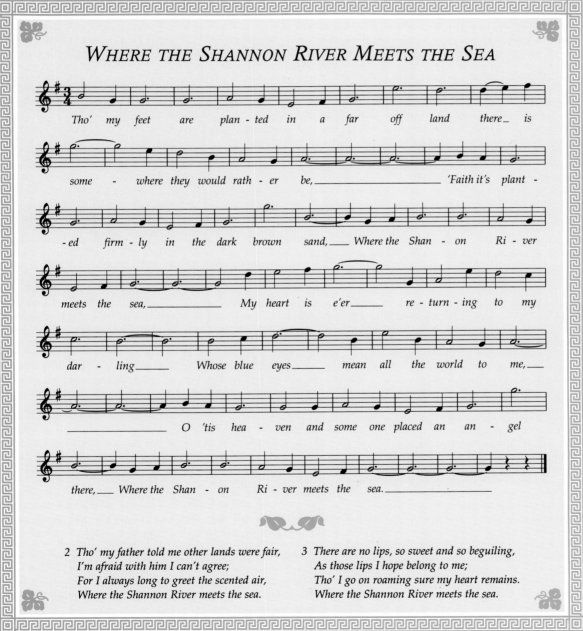

WHERE THE SHANNON RIVER MEETS THE SEA

Tho' my feet are plan-ted in a far off land there is some-where they would rath-er be, 'Faith it's plant-ed firm-ly in the dark brown sand, Where the Shan-on Ri-ver meets the sea, My heart is e'er re-turn-ing to my dar-ling Whose blue eyes mean all the world to me, O 'tis hea-ven and some one placed an an-gel there, Where the Shan-on Ri-ver meets the sea.

2 Tho' my father told me other lands were fair,
I'm afraid with him I can't agree;
For I always long to greet the scented air,
Where the Shannon River meets the sea.

3 There are no lips, so sweet and so beguiling,
As those lips I hope belong to me;
Tho' I go on roaming sure my heart remains.
Where the Shannon River meets the sea.

CONTAE MHUIGHEO

The County Mayo

ABOVE: *Raftery's simple headstone stands in Killeeneen, Co. Galway.*

BELOW: *'The wide plains of Mayo ....' Doo Lough near Delphi, Co. Mayo*

Raftery, the Gaelic poet and author of the song 'Contae Mhuigheo', was born in Killeadan near Kiltimagh in Co. Mayo in 1779. As a boy he lost his sight, but grew up with a gift for making poetry and song. He also became a fiddle player and these accomplishments made his living for him. His immediate patrons were the Taaffe family of the Big House at Killeadan.

While still a young man, Raftery left his native Mayo, faced southwards, and spent the rest of his life in Co. Galway, in the Athenry, Loughrea, Gort and Craughwell area, where he died in 1835.

Raftery's songs were composed for the people he met in his wanderings around the Galway countryside and they were handed down from generation to generation in oral tradition. The fact that they have survived until today shows the impact the poet made on his audience.

In his songs Raftery remembered his friends and patrons, celebrating their good times, lamenting their misfortunes. He held an acrimonious discourse with his old friend whiskey, vowing never to touch the stuff again, but it seems reconciliation was achieved to their mutual satisfaction.

Love also stirred the poetic heart and soul of the blind poet and his passionate verses for the beautiful Mary Hynes of Ballylee, near Gort, are still quoted in the original and in translation:

> *She is the sky of the sun, she is the dart of love;*
> *She is the love of my heart, she is a rune;*
> *She is above the women of the race of Eve;*
> *As the sun is above the moon.*

Little did Raftery know that nearly one hundred years later, another poet, the Nobel prizewinner for literature, William Butler Yeats, would come to live in the ancient tower-house of Ballylee (Thoor Ballylee), and could still listen to the local people talking in whispers about Raftery and Mary Hynes. At first Yeats failed to understand how a blind man could write so passionately about the beauty of a woman, but in his own poem, 'The Tower', Yeats found the answer in an ancient precedent:

> *Strange, but the man who made the song was blind;*
> *Yet, now I have considered it, I find*
> *That nothing strange; the tragedy began*
> *With Homer that was a blind man.*

Raftery's 'Contae Mhuigheo', though in one sense a song of exile, is more a celebration of his own county, a celebration of his own place. He gives luscious descriptions of the Mayo landscape, its abundant crops, its wildlife, its rivers and lakes, teeming with fish, its pastures full of sheep and cattle, its woods full of deer. He paints an environmental paradise presided over by a generous people who welcome all strangers with food and drink and shelter, but this song is also full of the joys and the promise of spring. Many poets have translated 'Contae Mhuigheo': certainly James Stephens captures the spirit of the original.

So anyone visiting the west of Ireland should take in Raftery's wild plains of Mayo with Kiltimagh in the centre, Castlebar in the west and Claremorris in the south. This indeed is poets' country. Near Gort is Coole Park, the home of Lady Gregory, a friend of Yeats, and a hostess to many famous writers. Further on is Tullira Castle, near Ardrahan, the home of Edward Martyn, another writer of the great Irish

CONTAE MHUIGHEO

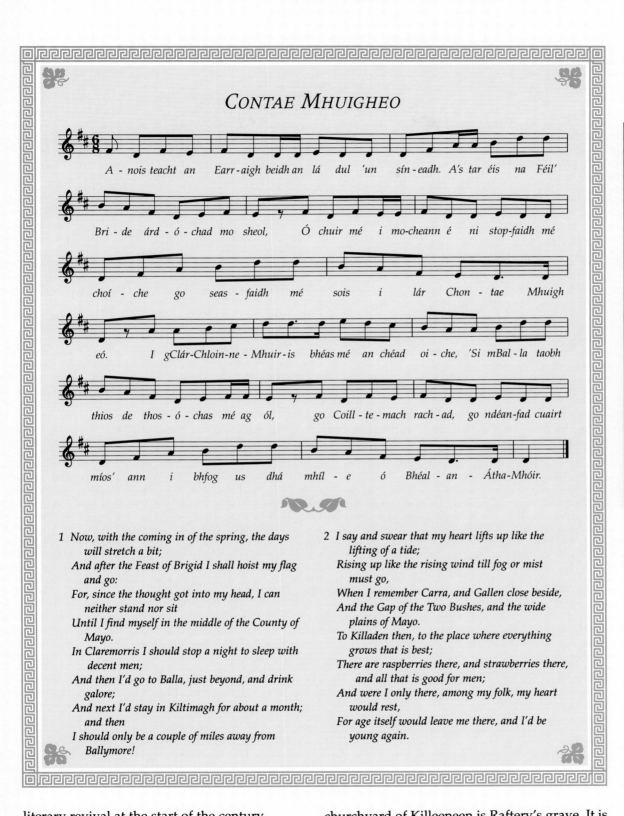

A - nois teacht an Earr-aigh beidh an lá dul 'un sín-eadh. A's tar éis na Féil'
Bri - de árd - ó - chad mo sheol, Ó chuir mé i mo-cheann é ni stop-faidh mé
choí - che go seas-faidh mé sois i lár Chon - tae Mhuigh
eó. I gClár-Chloin-ne - Mhuir-is bhéas mé an chéad oi - che, 'Si mBal - la taobh
thios de thos - ó - chas mé ag ól, go Coill - te - mach rach - ad, go ndéan-fad cuairt
míos' ann i bhfog us dhá mhíl - e ó Bhéal - an - Átha-Mhóir.

1 Now, with the coming in of the spring, the days
    will stretch a bit;
And after the Feast of Brigid I shall hoist my flag
    and go:
For, since the thought got into my head, I can
    neither stand nor sit
Until I find myself in the middle of the County of
    Mayo.
In Claremorris I should stop a night to sleep with
    decent men;
And then I'd go to Balla, just beyond, and drink
    galore;
And next I'd stay in Kiltimagh for about a month;
    and then
I should only be a couple of miles away from
    Ballymore!

2 I say and swear that my heart lifts up like the
    lifting of a tide;
Rising up like the rising wind till fog or mist
    must go,
When I remember Carra, and Gallen close beside,
And the Gap of the Two Bushes, and the wide
    plains of Mayo.
To Killaden then, to the place where everything
    grows that is best;
There are raspberries there, and strawberries there,
    and all that is good for men;
And were I only there, among my folk, my heart
    would rest,
For age itself would leave me there, and I'd be
    young again.

ABOVE: the monument to
Raftery on the village
green in Craughwell

literary revival at the start of the century.

And still in that area, do visit Craughwell, where you can see monuments to Lady Gregory and Raftery, and not too far away in the old churchyard of Killeeneen is Raftery's grave. It is marked with a headstone erected there at the turn of the century by Lady Gregory, Yeats and their literary friends. *CMcM*

THE BANKS OF MY OWN LOVELY LEE

Growing up in Macroom, I had the good fortune to call two storied and sung-about rivers my own. The Sullán flows outside the Ó Riada front door in Irish-speaking Cúil Aodha and, ten miles east just before joining the Lee, it meanders behind the garden of my childhood at the eastern end of the long town of Macroom. We swam in the pools of the Sullán and caught tiny fish with jam jars.

Less than half-an-hour's walk from the town, over the high hill of Sleveen, lay the swampy river-forest of the Gearagh through which flowed the Lee in myriad channels. This inland delta is still, even in its transformed post-hydro-electric-flooding state, remarkable for its exotic plant life. In earlier centuries it was a haven for such legendary outlaws as Seán Rua, and in my boyhood a sanctuary for poteen-makers. There we fished for roach, and it was the perfect terrain for games of 'explorers and savages'. That's where we 'sported and played', though not perhaps in ways envisaged in the song, and by stretches of river that were a far cry from the Mardyke and the ill-fated elm trees.

The Lee, which the seventh-century monk St Finbarr traversed from his scenic retreat in Gougane Barra to the estuarial head water where he founded his monastic school, is an essential symbol of Cork, county and city. But it is the urban river valley – in Spenser's lines:

'The spreading Lee that like an island fayre
Encloseth Cork with his divided flood'

that is really sung about in the 'anthem'. The promenade of the Mardyke is at its centre, its line of elm trees as dead and gone as the long-ago courting couples who were discouraged from perpendicular dalliance by the sticky creosote liberally applied to the barks by order of puritanical city fathers.

The 'banks' of the song extend westward along the Lee fields to 'sweet Inniscarra' and eastward towards the harbour down the Marina to Blackrock, with the dominating heights (geographical and social) of Montenotte and Tivoli across the river.

Who wrote the words of 'The Banks'? It's the kind of question that would keep Cork pub circles happily engaged for hours, but no wiser thereafter. Contrary to popular impression in Cork, the author wasn't John Fitzgerald, the 'Bard of the Lee', author of another local favourite, the rather syrupy 'Beautiful City'. Other evidence may indicate an emigrant Irish-American provenance, while what might be called a Fenian note is struck in one of the two verses that are rarely sung.

Whatever the authorship, 'The Banks' was a popular Cork ballad in the last quarter of the nineteenth century, but the air to which it is now sung would seem to be a surprisingly modern one. In 1933, the actor-manager Dick Forbes asked James Charles Shanahan, organist, composer and a member of a distinguished musical family, to put music to 'The Banks' for a Forbes show in the Opera House in Cork. And so it came to pass. Shanahan published the 'copyright' music sheet in 1935 and singers like Martin Dempsey and Seán Ó Siocháin helped to popularise the new 'anthem'. Before long, it had totally replaced former favourites such as 'The Bells of Shandon'.

'The Banks' stops short of being maudlin but is heavily nostalgic, as befits a tribe that is homesick even when it is at home. Most important, the song gives everyone a chance to join in (twice!) harmoniously and full-throatedly in the concluding two lines of the two verses that are generally sung.

For all its flaws and its vulnerability to irreverent punning and parodying, 'The Banks' has the established stature of an anthem, albeit one mainly for export. By a kind of tacit protocol, it is rarely rendered in Cork sing-songs at home. It is best heard in bars in the

FAR RIGHT: 'the green mossy banks and wild flowers ….' Cork spring

BELOW: a chapel beside Gougane Barra, the lake source of the River Lee

THE BANKS OF MY OWN LOVELY LEE

Oh how oft do my thoughts in their fan-cy take flight, to the scenes of my child-hood a - way,___ To the days when each pa - tri-ot's vis - ion seemed bright, ere I dreamed that those joys should de - cay,___ When my heart was as light as the wild winds that blow, down the Mar-dyke through each elm___ tree,___ Where I sport - ed and played 'neath each green lea - fy shade, On the banks of my own love - ly Lee___ Where I sport - ed and played 'neath each green lea - fy shade, On the banks of my own love - ly Lee.___

2 And then in the springtime of laughter and song,
    Can I ever forget the sweet hours
    With the friends of my youth as we rambled along
    'Mongst the green mossy banks and wild flowers.
    Then too, when the evening sun's sinking to rest
    Sheds its golden light over the sea
    The maid with her lover the wild daisies pressed
    On the banks of my own lovely Lee.
    The maid with her lover the wild daisies pressed
    On the banks of my own lovely Lee.

ABOVE: 'the maid with her lover the wild daisies pressed ....'

BELOW: the banks of the leafy River Lee at Cork in early spring

vicinity of Croke Park on All-Ireland days, or sweetest of all, when rousingly raised in Semple Stadium and in Thurles pubs after a victory in the Munster Final.

Yerra, you can't bate 'The Banks', boy!   JM

CARRIGDHOUN

'Why don't you write more songs?' was Thomas Davis's enthusiastic reaction to the publication, in the *Nation* on 15 February 1845, of Denny Lane's composition, 'Lament of the Irish Maiden: A Brigade Ballad' or 'Carrigdhoun' as it was soon to be popularly titled. Praise indeed!

There is an inexpressible Cork resonance about the name Denny Lane. He was born in 1818 into a wealthy Cork distilling family, earned a Master of Arts degree at Trinity College Dublin, and was called to the Bar after studies at the Inner Temple, London. He was caught up in the romantic nationalism of the Young Ireland movement and contributed to the pages of the *Nation* under the pen name of 'Domhnall Gleannach'. Though by no means a revolutionary subversive, he was suspect enough to the authorities to be jailed without

BELOW: *Owenabue River as it approaches Crosshaven, Co. Cork*

trial in Cork prison for four months in 1848. This added to his reputation in later years as a sterling patriot, as did his friendship with Young Ireland 'greats' like Davis and Charles Gavan Duffy.

Lane was an outstanding entrepreneur of his time. A man of independent fortune, he prided himself on the well-rounded education he had received at Cork's classical schools. He deplored the snobbish tendency of the Cork bourgeoisie to send their scions across the Irish Sea to acquire 'an electroplated English accent'. Indeed. Weren't their own plummy native woodnotes good enough for them?

The Owenabue (*Abhainn Bhuí* or Yellow River) is a modestly short stream, no more than ten or twelve miles long, that runs into the harbour at Crosshaven, near Cork. 'Angry' it is not, even in the depths of winter, though it may become mildly irritated at times. The place-names in the song, Carrigdhoun (*carraig donn*, 'brown rock') and Ard-na-Lee (*ard na laoi*, 'Lee height') are the author's inventions, though they may correspond to particular features of the landscape. It is a remarkable tribute to the song's popularity over the years that the fictional place-name of Carrigdhoun is alive and well, and proudly borne by a local newspaper, a pottery co-op, a hurling team and an oil company (a modestly small one, doubtless!).

Denny Lane would have been charmed.

The song belongs to a well-known genre made popular by the *Nation*. The physical setting is lushly romantic, as is the relationship between the maiden and her 'Domhnall dhu'(*Dónal dubh*, 'dark-haired Donal'). The young man loves both her and Ireland, but in the general post-Jacobite ruin he has joined the Irish Brigade in the French service – in the *Nation* tradition, a highly glamorised occupation.

The haunting air and the simple sentiments have had a perennial appeal for generations of Cork people. It was published in successive editions of the immensely successful book of songs and poems *Spirit of the Nation*, and Lane's obituary in 1895 mentions that the song was popular then 'and is likely to remain so'.

'Carrigdhoun' is taught in school and sung in parlours and pubs. Theoretically a woman's song, in practice it is rendered with gusto by both sexes, lending itself to gorgeous harmonising. And its author is not forgotten. When he died, his obituarist mournfully observed that in a busy life, Lane's productions 'were entirely fugitive', or ephemeral. What a rich irony! If he had written a shelf of scholarly tomes, he would not be as well, and certainly not as fondly, remembered. Whenever 'Carrigdhoun' is sung today, the chances are that someone in the company will shake a head in nostalgic admiration and murmur, Cork-style, 'Ah, Denny Lane, boy, Denny Lane'. You could be forgiven for thinking the reference was to a recently deceased friend rather than to the Cork merchant who penned 'Carrigdhoun' a century and a half ago.

Oh to be remembered just like that!   JM

ABOVE: Cork City Gaol, where Denny Lane was once incarcerated

BELOW: Denny Lane, a well-loved Cork man of the nineteenth century

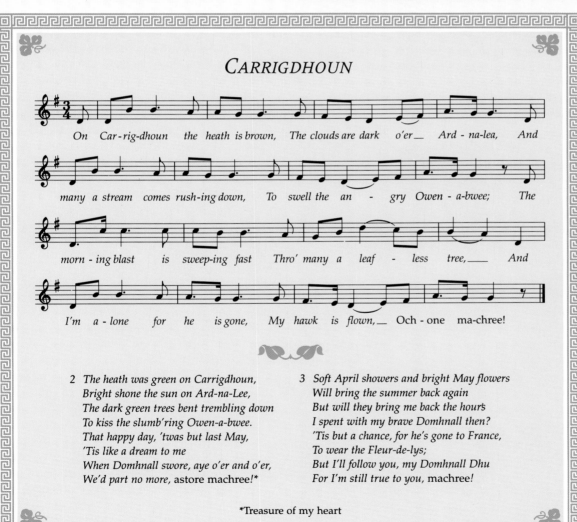

CARRIGDHOUN

On Carrigdhoun the heath is brown, The clouds are dark o'er Ardnalea, And many a stream comes rushing down, To swell the angry Owen-a-bwee; The morning blast is sweeping fast Thro' many a leafless tree, And I'm alone for he is gone, My hawk is flown, Ochone ma-chree!

2 The heath was green on Carrigdhoun,
   Bright shone the sun on Ard-na-Lee,
   The dark green trees bent trembling down
   To kiss the slumb'ring Owen-a-bwee.
   That happy day, 'twas but last May,
   'Tis like a dream to me
   When Domhnall swore, aye o'er and o'er,
   We'd part no more, astore machree!*

3 Soft April showers and bright May flowers
   Will bring the summer back again
   But will they bring me back the hours
   I spent with my brave Domhnall then?
   'Tis but a chance, for he's gone to France,
   To wear the Fleur-de-lys;
   But I'll follow you, my Domhnall Dhu
   For I'm still true to you, machree!

*Treasure of my heart

I'M SITTIN' ON THE STILE, MARY

The Irish Emigrant

Popular ballads can emerge from strange and unlikely backgrounds and unlikely people. The joys and sorrows of Irish country folk are generally looked for in the songs of a local poet whose name is normally anonymous. But the author of our song came from a very different social position and was far from anonymous. In fact she was a titled lady twice over.

Helen Selina Sheridan (1807-67) did not find the gift of poetry on the side of the road. She was the granddaughter of Richard Brinsley Sheridan, the celebrated Irish dramatist, and her sister, Caroline Norton and her son, Frederick, Marquis of Dufferin, were also well-known writers. At the age of eighteen she married the Hon. Price Blackwood, later Lord Dufferin, and so became Lady Dufferin. Lord Dufferin died in 1841 and she remained a widow until 1862 when she married the Earl of Gifford and so became the Countess of Gifford.

All this seems a strange background for the author of a popular sentimental Irish ballad, but in the introduction to *The Reciter's Treasury of Irish Verse and Prose*, Alfred Perceval Graves (author of 'Father O'Fym') has this to say about her in explanation:

> Lady Dufferin excels her sister in the sheer artlessness of her art. The simplest themes seem to attract her most. Living a happy domestic life amid Irish surroundings, her warm heart beats in such close sympathy with her peasant neighbours that in 'I'm Sittin' on the Stile, Mary', and 'The Bay of Dublin', she writes as if she were one of them, and adds to that inspiration a felicity of phrase which is lacking in the earlier Anglo-Irish hedge poets or street ballad writers, and only begins to recur again in the writings of William Allingham, and now and then in those of Edward Walsh, Thomas Davis, and Sir Samuel Ferguson.

'I'm Sittin' on the Stile, Mary' was indeed popular all over the English-speaking world and particularly in America: it appeared both in major anthologies and in penny songbooks and was a regular on the concert platform. It came out on gramophone records by various Irish tenors including, of course, John McCormack. A further proof of its popularity, if any be needed, is the fact that it was parodied in cheap little music-hall songbooks published in New York at the end of the nineteenth century. Something has to be very well known indeed to become the subject of a parody.

> I'm sittin' on the stile, Mary
> Away up in the mines
> A lookin' out for lumps of gold
> And pockets all I find
> But the lumps I find is precious small
> And very few at that
> And I feel that I have been, Mary
> A most almighty flat.

This song belongs to no one place in Ireland but to the whole country from Donegal to Wexford, from Antrim to Kerry. For lots of people, particularly those far away from home 'I'm Sittin' on the Stile, Mary' will evoke many nostalgic memories.

CMcM

BELOW FAR RIGHT: 'the little church stands near....' Ballintoy, Co. Antrim

BELOW: James Glen Wilson's 'Emigrant Ship Leaving Belfast'

I'm Sittin' on the Stile, Mary

I'm sit-tin' on the stile Ma-ry where we sat side by side, On a
bright May morn-ing long a-go when first you were my bride, The corn was spring-ing
fresh and green and the lark sang loud and high, And the red was on your lip Ma-ry and the
love-light in your eye, The place is lit-tle changed Ma-ry, the day is bright as
then, The lark's loud song is in my ear and the corn is green a-gain, But I
miss the soft clasp of your hand and your breath warm on my cheek. And I still keep list-'ning
for the words you ne-ver more may speak, You ne-ver more may speak.

2 'Tis but a step down yonder lane,
The little church stands near –
The church where we were wed, Mary –
I see the spire from here;
But the graveyard lies between, Mary,
My step might break your rest,
Where you, my darling, lie asleep
With your baby on your breast.

3 I'm very lonely now, Mary,
The poor make no new friends;
But, oh, they love the better still
The few our Father sends.
And you were all I had, Mary,
My blessing and my pride;
There's nothing left to care for now
Since my poor Mary died.

4 Yours was the good, brave heart, Mary,
That still kept hoping on,
When trust in God had left my soul,
And half my strength was gone.
There was comfort ever on your lip,
And the kind look on your brow;
I bless you, Mary, for that same,
Though you can't hear me now.

5 I'm bidding you a long farewell,
My Mary, kind and true!
But I'll not forget you, darling,
In the land I'm going to.
They say there's bread and work for all,
And the sun shines always there;
But I'll not forget old Ireland
Were it fifty times as fair.

THE BLACKBIRD OF SWEET AVONDALE

The 'blackbird' of the song was no avian songster but Charles Stewart Parnell. This ballad, in the tradition of the Caoine (Irish female lament), was written in 1881 by his sister, Fanny Parnell, founder of the Ladies' Land League. Its occasion was the imprisonment of Parnell for his involvement in the Land War and his condemnation of Gladstone's Land Act, passed the same year. Part of its appeal lies in the bringing together of two of the places most often associated with Parnell's memory: Kilmainham Jail in Dublin, and Avondale, Co. Wicklow, one-time home of the Parnell family.

Drawing on two well-known Jacobite relics, 'The Blackbird' and 'Lady Albany's Lament for King Charles', which bemoan the dispossession and exile of King Charles II, Fanny Parnell invested her ballad with the regality of the earlier songs and in so doing, forged a link between Ireland's uncrowned Stewart Parnell and England's displaced Stuart. Unknowingly, she also captured what were to become the essential aspects of the Parnell legend: love, betrayal, and in the symbol of the blackbird, the lone voice of leadership. In the popular imagination, the sad female strain '... where is

ABOVE: Fanny, Charles Stewart Parnell's beautiful and supportive sister

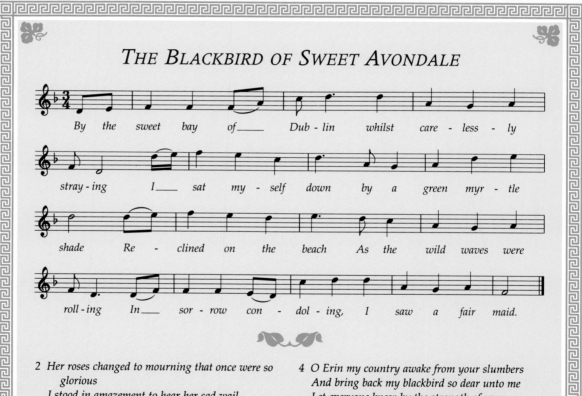

THE BLACKBIRD OF SWEET AVONDALE

By the sweet bay of Dub-lin whilst care-less-ly stray-ing I sat my-self down by a green myr-tle shade Re-clined on the beach As the wild waves were roll-ing In sor-row con-dol-ing, I saw a fair maid.

2 Her roses changed to mourning that once were so
   glorious
   I stood in amazement to hear her sad wail.
   Her heart strings burst out in wild accents
   uproarious
   Saying, where is my Blackbird of sweet Avondale?

3 The cold prison dungeon is no habitation
   For one to his country so loyal and true
   So give him his freedom without hesitation
   Remember he fought hard for freedom and you.

4 O Erin my country awake from your slumbers
   And bring back my blackbird so dear unto me
   Let everyone know by the strength of your
   numbers
   That we as a nation would like to be free.

5 O heaven! Give ear to my supplication
   And strengthen the bold sons of old Grainne
   Mhaoil
   And grant that my country will soon be a nation
   And bring back my blackbird to sweet Avondale.

ABOVE: Parnell's portrait hangs in pride of place at Avondale House today.

my Blackbird of sweet Avondale' calls to mind the renowned affair of Parnell and Katharine (Kitty) O'Shea and its cruel exploitation in 1890 by Parnell's political opponents.

Just a mile from the village of Rathdrum (Ring Fort of the Ridge), 'Sweet' Avondale is situated at the southern end of one of Wicklow's most beautiful vales, the Avonmore. The 530-acre estate, originally known as 'Hayesville' after its first owner, Samuel Hayes, is famed not only as the birthplace of Parnell but for its other great glory – trees. It was Hayes, a tree enthusiast, who planted the estate's oldest surviving species, the beech, in the late eighteenth century. Through a century of Parnell possession the planting and cultivation continued and when, in 1904, a few years after 'The Chief's' death, the estate was taken over by the British government, Avondale became the State Forestry School. Under the directorship of A.C. Forbes, a forest garden – a series of experimental square acre plots consisting of some forty different species – was laid out. Forbes' Grove, which features some rare pine and rhododendron specimens, commemorates his planting. Some of the most exotic trees are on the banks of the Avonmore River which passes through the estate on its way to the Meeting of the Waters in the Vale of Avoca, just two miles south of Avondale. As the ochre river flows by, tinged from its journey through the richly mineralled rock of south-east Wicklow, its music blends softly with the graceful sweeping of nearby hemlock and the high 'whispering' of giant sequoia.

In its heyday, prior to the successful cultivation of the trees, Avondale House, built on an eminence near the river, held a commanding view of the valley, of the Cullentragh and Kirikee mountains to the west

and Trooperstown Hill to the east. Square and rather ordinary looking, the house, which is not glimpsed until one turns the last bend of the impressive driveway, is at first a bit disappointing. However, some have read its austere, solid appearance as befitting the home of a leader of Parnell's character, an issue, amongst others, hotly debated each year in the Parnell Summer School which takes place at Avondale.

There are various versions of this ballad and various airs to accompany them. As a testimony perhaps to the lasting power of Parnell's leadership, it is interesting to note that in a different ballad, written after his death and titled simply 'Avondale', the Blackbird of Sweet Avondale has become an eagle:

'Oh have you been to Avondale,
And lingered in its lovely vale.
Where tall trees whisper and know the tale
Of Avondale's proud eagle?'
AK

ABOVE: autumn sunlight in the glorious forests of Avondale estate

FAR LEFT: Avondale House, Co. Wicklow, once home to Charles Stewart Parnell

KILCASH

The stately ruins of the great Butler stronghold of Cill Chais (Kilcash) has sung its name with profound affection into the imaginations of generations of Irish people who learned the song at school and later, perhaps, came upon the striking translation by Frank O'Connor.

You come to Cill Chais over the mountain from Callan in Co. Kilkenny, or along the valley of the Suir through Kilsheelan from Carrick-on-Suir or Clonmel. The impressive tower house stands on the southern slopes of Sliabh na mBan, close by the sequestered village of the same name, and fulfils the expectations evoked by the song. To reach it is more a sense of recognition, a 'living back into' something long known and deeply felt, rather than a mere arrival or discovery. This once proud castle, built in the sixteenth century and situated above one of the richest tracts of land in Ireland, is linked inextricably with the haunting words and plaintive air which concentrate a deep emotional experience of upheaval and transformation.

FAR RIGHT: 'And a darkness falling from heaven ....' Kilcash

BELOW: moonrise over the ruins of Kilcash Castle, Co. Kilkenny

The song harks back to the days of Lady Iveagh who died in 1744 and whose name was synonymous with kindness. She was Margaret Burke, daughter of William, Earl of Clanrickard and Lady Helen MacCarthy, daughter of the Earl of Clancarthy. She first married Brian Magennis, the First Viscount of Iveagh in County Down, who fought on King James' side at the Battle of the Boyne. Following his death she married Thomas Butler of Kilcash, who had also fought on the Jacobite side at the Battle of Aughrim. The Kilcash household was strongly Catholic. Priests had been ordained there and it was a place of refuge in Penal times for her brother-in-law, Christopher Butler, the Catholic Archbishop of Cashel. For the people of the district the household was a source of hope and consolation during a time of harsh religious suppression and cultural alienation.

The castle retains an air of defiant splendour: one can readily imagine those once-great woods around it, destined to be felled at the end of the eighteenth century. By then the family had conformed to the Established Church and Walter Butler, Earl of Ormond, owner of Kilcash, now a lord of the new United Kingdom, left for England.

The immediate occasion of doom-burdened 'Cill Chais' was the felling of the woods and the later dismantling of the castle. But in recalling the lost glory of that household, renowned for its fidelity and generosity, the song invests the name of Cill Chais with a symbolic power that evokes a wider and deeply shared experience of universal loss, emphasised by its vain yearning for 'long dances danced in the garden, fiddle music and mirth among men'. *EÓhA*

KILCASH

Anon. (18th century). Translated from the Irish by Frank O'Connor

Cad a dhéan - fai - mid feas - ta gan adh - mad? Tá
Ah!___ what shall we do___ for tim - ber? The

dei - re na gcoillt' ar lár___ Nil__ tracht ar Chill Chais ná a
last of the woods_ is down,___ Kil - cash and the house of its

teagh - lach, 'Sni cluin - fear a cling go bráth___ An___
glo - ry, And the bells of the house are gone.___ The___

áit úd 'na gcómh-nuiodh an deigh - bhean Fuair gra - dam is meidhir thar
Spot where that la - dy wait - ed who shamed all wo - men for

mhnaibh,___ Bhiodh_ iar - laí a' tar - raing thar
grace,___ When__ earls___ came sail - ing to

tuinn ann, 'San t-Aif - reann binn dá rádh.___
greet her, And Mass___ was said in that place.

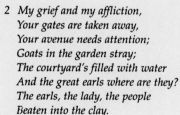

2 My grief and my affliction,
   Your gates are taken away,
   Your avenue needs attention;
   Goats in the garden stray;
   The courtyard's filled with water
   And the great earls where are they?
   The earls, the lady, the people
   Beaten into the clay.

3 No sound of duck or geese there,
   Hawk's cry or eagle's call,
   No humming of the bees there
   That brought honey and wax for all,
   Not even the song of the birds there
   When the sun has gone down in the west,
   Nor a cuckoo on top of the boughs there,
   Singing the world to rest.

4 There's mist there tumbling from branches
   Unstirred by night and by day,
   And a darkness falling from heaven,
   And our fortunes have ebbed away;
   There's no holly nor hazel nor ash there;
   The pasture is rock and stone,
   The crown of the forest is withered
   And the last of its game is gone.

5 I beseech of Mary and Jesus
   That the great come home again.
   With long dances danced in the garden,
   Fiddle music and mirth among men,
   That Kilcash, the home of our fathers,
   Be lifted on high again,
   And from that to the deluge of waters
   In bounty and peace remain.

ABOVE: the shield of the Butlers, one of the great Anglo-Norman families

BELOW: an engraving of an eighteenth-century itinerant fiddler

THE OLD ORANGE FLUTE

Gavan Duffy, who compiled *Ballad Poetry of Ireland*, a collection of ballads concerned with the nationalist spirit of Ireland, in his introduction declared that some Orange texts had to be included because:

> '...whatever could illustrate the character, passions or opinions of any class of Irishmen, that we gladly adopted ... [the Orange songs] echo faithfully the sentiments of a strong, vehement and indomitable body of Irishmen'.

Later in the nineteenth century the poet W. B. Yeats also seems to have been influenced by both nationalist and Orange popular rhymes. It was as late as the 1880s when he discovered nationalist balladry, but he had admired Orange balladry much earlier: an old Orange song book which he read as a child in a hayloft in Sligo gave him 'the pleasure of rhyme for the first time' and inspired him with a desire to die 'fighting the Fenians'.

The Orangemen of Ireland, who want to keep political and religious links with Britain, also want to preserve their cultural identity. Nevertheless, their songs and nationalist songs share many elements: the colloquial language, for instance, similar themes and identical tunes.

However, 'The Old Orange Flute' is a song all on its own. It is a parody of an Orange song and could just as easily be a parody of a nationalist song. In whatever camp it is sung it inevitably provokes laughter.

It pursues the theme of betrayal and the role of the turncoat to extremity and absurdity. The narrative proceeds in a series of graphic images, like a movie cartoon, tossing in stereotypes and

ABOVE: an Orangeman during the annual Twelfth of July celebrations

RIGHT: Sir John Lavery's painting 'The Twelfth of July in Portadown'

tribal characteristics accurately and deftly, as if in some paradoxical fashion both streams of Irish political and religious verse are flowing in the one direction.

It was a favourite party piece of the late Cardinal Tomás O Fiaich: he always sang it with humour and it appeared as if the good nature of the song might heal some of the wounds of a riven community. Certainly there was always a sense of something stronger than wistfulness charging the atmosphere as he threw his head back and his face creased in smiles. *DH*

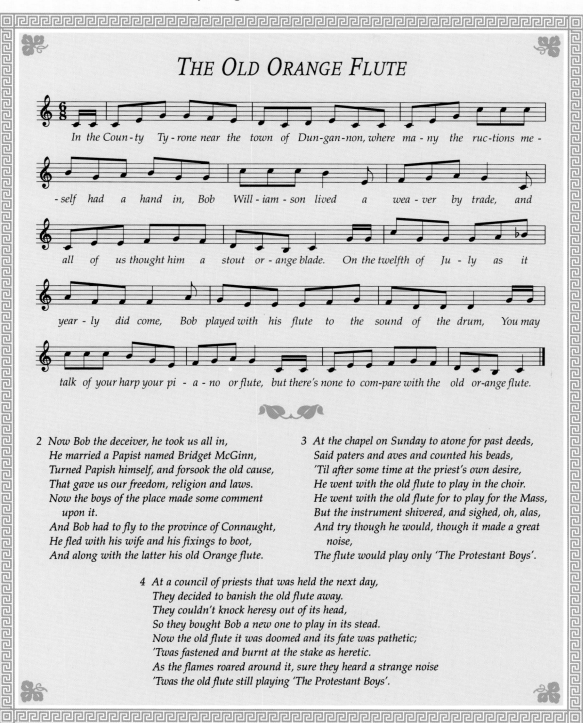

THE OLD ORANGE FLUTE

In the Coun-ty Ty-rone near the town of Dun-gan-non, where ma-ny the ruc-tions me-self had a hand in, Bob Will-iam-son lived a wea-ver by trade, and all of us thought him a stout or-ange blade. On the twelfth of Ju-ly as it year-ly did come, Bob played with his flute to the sound of the drum, You may talk of your harp your pi-a-no or flute, but there's none to com-pare with the old or-ange flute.

2 Now Bob the deceiver, he took us all in,
   He married a Papist named Bridget McGinn,
   Turned Papish himself, and forsook the old cause,
   That gave us our freedom, religion and laws.
   Now the boys of the place made some comment
      upon it.
   And Bob had to fly to the province of Connaught,
   He fled with his wife and his fixings to boot,
   And along with the latter his old Orange flute.

3 At the chapel on Sunday to atone for past deeds,
   Said paters and aves and counted his beads,
   'Til after some time at the priest's own desire,
   He went with the old flute to play in the choir.
   He went with the old flute for to play for the Mass,
   But the instrument shivered, and sighed, oh, alas,
   And try though he would, though it made a great
      noise,
   The flute would play only 'The Protestant Boys'.

4 At a council of priests that was held the next day,
   They decided to banish the old flute away.
   They couldn't knock heresy out of its head,
   So they bought Bob a new one to play in its stead.
   Now the old flute it was doomed and its fate was pathetic;
   'Twas fastened and burnt at the stake as heretic.
   As the flames roared around it, sure they heard a strange noise
   'Twas the old flute still playing 'The Protestant Boys'.

ABOVE: *a detail of a 'fluter' from William Conor's painting 'The Twelfth'*

THE HARP THAT ONCE

Thomas Moore was born in Dublin on 28 May 1779 and is best remembered for the songs he wrote which were published under the title, *Moore's Melodies*. They are extremely beautiful in their composition, the words fitting snugly into the tunes, very adventurous in the rhythms they choose, yet startling in their simplicity.

The eighteenth century in Ireland had started with commercial success and proceeded with glamour. This was the time in which Dublin grew into the second city of the British Empire, when its Englishness was expressed in the elegant terraces and squares of the city's architecture. There was enormous prosperity for the land-owning classes, the merchants, the professionals and the administrators, but the vast bulk of the people lived in dire poverty.

It was towards the end of the 1700s that things began to go wrong and the country began to run less smoothly. Eventually there was a rebellion against the government in 1798 by the United Irishmen, who had drawn inspiration from the revolutions in France and America. The rising failed, and in the aftermath Ireland lost her own parliament and was governed from London after the Act of Union in 1800. Commerce dwindled and prosperity diminished, even for the privileged classes. For the millions of poor people things just got worse.

So all the heady feeling of nationhood, the glimpses of liberty and brotherhood, were lost after the failure of the rising and the loss of a parliament. The old order was finished and defeat seemed final. Tom Moore's patriotic songs tell of 'the glory that is gone'. All during the nineteenth century it was Moore's stirring songs with their banners and crowns, harps and round towers and collars of gold, that provided the potent icons of Irish patriotism.

Moore had written these lyrics to tunes collected from traditional sources by the northern musician Edward Bunting. He drew freely from the melodies that Bunting had taken down, in the first instance from ancient harpers at the Belfast Harp Festival in 1792 and later from traditional musicians all over Ireland.

Moore's songs were on everyone's lips. He had gone to live in England after he graduated from Trinity College Dublin in 1801; but when he returned to Ireland he was greeted as the Beatles were in the 1960s – when he went to the theatre the play stopped and didn't start again until he had walked on to the stage and addressed the audience; when he travelled from Dublin to Limerick the roads were lined with his admirers. As Lord Byron wrote:

> ' ... Moore had a peculiarity of talent, or rather talents – poetry, music, voice, all his own; and an expression in each, which never was, and never will be, possessed by another. But he is capable of higher flights in poetry. There is nothing Moore may not do ...'

Although Tom Moore has often been mocked by those who have seen him as a dandy who surrendered his pride and nationality to English patronage, a great number of writers have

BELOW: *Hill of Tara, Co. Meath, the religious centre of ancient Ireland*

THE HARP THAT ONCE

The harp that once thro' Ta-ra's Halls the soul of mu-sic shed, Now hangs as mute on Ta-ra's Walls as if that soul were fled, So sleeps the pride of for-mer days so glo-ry's thrill is o'er, And hearts that once beat high for praise now feel that pulse no more.

2 *No more to chiefs and ladies bright,*
The harp of Tara swells.
The chord alone, that breaks at night,
Its tale of ruin tells.
The freedom now so seldom wakes,
The only throb she gives,
Is when some heart indignant breaks,
To show that still she lives.

ABOVE: 'the harp of Tara swells ....' Many medieval harpists were blind.

BELOW: Mound of the Hostages at the Tara Interpretation Centre

admired him and his work. James Joyce, for instance, often sang his songs and referred to them in his own writing – 'Erin, the Tear and the Smile', 'The Harp That Once', 'The Minstrel Boy', 'Oft in the Stilly Night', Love's Young Dream' and many others. He died in Wiltshire in England in February 1852. When the English poet John Betjeman visited his grave there he wrote:

'I can regard you but neglected and poor
Dear bard of my childhood, mellifluous Moore,
That far from the land which of all you loved best,
In a village of England your bones should have rest.'
DH

THE KILRUDDERY HUNT

Despite the constant growth of population in Dublin and the inevitable urban sprawl, one is always reassuringly aware of the foothills of the Dublin and Wicklow mountains nuzzling the southern outskirts. This is true whether you see them at a distance from the gradually rising northside as you approach from the airport, take the more panoramic view from Dublin Bay so lovingly described in the closing pages of Brendan Behan's *Borstal Boy*, or catch a breathtaking glimpse of them along the vista of Merrion and Fitzwilliam squares. Their presence shapes the city into self-awareness and lifts the eye and heart.

Within a twenty minutes' drive from Dublin you find yourself surrounded by lush fields and hedges along winding roads that lead to those secluded and seductive glens that converge on the suburbs – Glencullen, Glencree and Glenasmole. One attractive turning from the mainstream traffic is at the Silver Tassie public house in Loughlinstown. Upon leaving the dual carriageway there is a gathering hush as you enter Cherrywood and Bride's Glen on the road to Kilternan and Enniskerry, a district which holds many antiquities. Despite the urban expansion it is still not impossible to visualise a foxhunt across this terrain, such as the one which took place in 1744 and is celebrated in this lilting tune.

On that particular day the hunt made its way as deep as Monkstown. Weston St John Joyce wrote in 1912 in *The Neighbourhood of Dublin* of the interesting allusions in the song to many places where, even then, foxhunting would be utterly impossible but which in the eighteenth century were wild and unenclosed – Carrickmines, Dalkey, Glenageary, Rochestown.

Nowadays one of the most accessible views of almost the whole course of the hunt would be from the summit of 800-foot-high Carrickgollagan Mountain, the site of the old lead mines, which you reach at Ballycorus along that quiet road from the Silver Tassie.   *EÓhA*

ABOVE: *terrain typical of the foothills of the Wicklow Mountains*

RIGHT: *a montage of the Kilruddery Hunt that hangs in Kilruddery House*

THE KILRUDDERY HUNT

In sev-en-teen hund-red and for-ty four, The fifth of De-cem-ber, I think 'twas no more, At five in the morn-ing, by most of the clocks, We rode from Kil-rud-dery in search of a fox. The Lough-lins-town land-lord, the brave O-wen Bray, And John-ny A-dair, too, were with us that day; Joe De-bil, Hal Pres-ton, those hunts-men so stout, Dick Holmes, some few oth-ers, and so we set out.

2 We cast off our hounds for an hour or more,
   When Wanton set up a most tuneable roar;
   'Hark, Wanton', cried Joe and the rest were not slack;
   For Wanton's no trifler, esteemed by the pack;
   Old Bounty and Collier came readily in,
   And every hound joined in the musical din:
   Had Diana been there, she'd been pleased to the life,
   And one of the lads got a goddess to wife.

3 Ten minutes past nine was the time of the day
   When Reynard broke cover, and this was his way –
   As strong from Killegar, as if he could fear none,
   Away he brush'd round by the house of Kilternan,
   To Carrickmines thence, and to Cherrywood then,
   Steep Shankhill he climbed, and to Ballyman glen,
   Bray Common he crossed, leap'd Lord Anglesey's wall,
   And seemed to say, 'Little I care for you all'.

4 He ran Bushes Grove tip to Carbury Byrnes –
   Joe Debil, Hal Preston, kept leading by turns;
   The earth it was open, yet he was so stout,
   Tho' he might have got in, still he chose to keep out;
   To Malpas high hills was the way that he flew,
   At Dalkey's stone common we had him in view;
   He drove on to Bullock, he slunk Glenageary,
   And so on to Monkstown, where Larry grew weary.

5 Thro' Rochestown wood like an arrow he passed,
   And came to the steep hills of Dalkey at last;
   There gallantly plunged himself into the sea,
   And said in his heart, 'None can now follow me'.
   But soon, to his cost, he perceived that no bounds
   Could stop the pursuit of the staunch-mettled hounds.
   His policy here did not serve him a rush,
   Five couples of Tartars were hard at his brush.

6 To recover the shore then again was his drift,
   But e'er he could reach to the top of the cliff,
   He found both of speed and of cunning a lack,
   Being way-laid and kill'd by the rest of the pack,
   At his death there were present the lads that I've sung,
   Save Lawry, who riding a garran was flung;
   Thus ended at length a most delicate chase,
   That held us five hours, and ten minutes' space.

THE OLD BOG ROAD

ABOVE: 'Bringing Home the Turf' by William Davis. The old bog road?

My first meeting with Teresa Brayton (1868-1943), who wrote 'The Old Bog Road', was in the fall of 1940 or the spring of 1941: I can't now be certain which, but the place, for sure, was the home of Brian O'Higgins, that old Republican sea-green incorruptible. On that occasion there was a dinner party followed by a musical evening. Or, more simply, people who could sing, sang.

Jimmy Broe sang. He had a fine tenor. He sang some Stephen Foster. Then he sang 'The Old Bog Road'. Now everybody from John McCormack to my uncle, Owen Gormley, way up there on the uncertain moorland border of Tyrone and Fermanagh, had, at some time or other, sung that song. But the point then was that the little silver-haired lady sitting by my side had written it: and by the time Jimmy got as far as 'So God be with you Ireland, and the Old Bog Road', the emotion in the room was vibrant, and the dear lady and myself were sitting hand-in-hand and a friendship had commenced that lasted until the day of her death.

That moment, half of a century ago, and that friendship all came back to me overwhelmingly when, a few years ago, I listened to a brilliant talk on John McCormack. For John McCormack meant as much, or more, to Teresa Brayton as he meant for decades to thousands of other Irish exiles. She told me how they had met in the States. From the great man himself I heard how he had made a point of seeking her out. For how could he pass on the road up above, as another song says, without coming in to find the woman who had written of 'the old bog road' and who spoke, as he sang, to the hearts of Irish exiles:

> Unto my own, the Irish, I send, with smiles and
>   tears,
> This little book of memories caught from the flying
>   years.
> With all the love within me and all the best I know,
> I'd call them o'er many a track to lands of long ago.

Those were the first lines in her first collection of poems, *Songs of the Dawn*, published in New York in 1913, and for her second collection, *The Flame of Ireland*, published in 1926, she wrote a brief and simple foreword: 'In offering this little book of verse to my kinsfolk, the Irish people, I ardently hope that it will find as warm a welcome to their hearts as did its predecessor …' It did too. Her chief concern was always for the exiles. She was one of them. It is in my memory that she told me that John McCormack told her the lines of hers he liked best were:

> 'I would know it in the darkness were I deaf and
>   dumb and blind,
> I would know it o'er the thrashing of a million
>   miles of foam,
> I would know it, sun or shadow, I would know it,
>   rain or wind,
> The road that leads to Ireland, the old road home.'

Later Teresa moved back to a pleasant house on the roadside between Kilcock and Enfield, just a little bit beyond the original of the old bog road. We walked that road together: it leads nowhere except into the heart of silence. When I say we, I mean Teresa and William Walsh, the elder brother of Michael Walsh, the poet, young Brian O'Higgins and myself. Regularly the three of us cycled to see her and enjoy her talk. She had known lots of people, notable and just ordinary like the rest of us, and observed them with a cool and kindly eye.

She died in that quiet midland country and lies at rest in the odd little graveyard of Cloncurry, a sort of crag or hillock to the right as you go westwards. One of the many good things I know about Anthony Cronin is that he stood by the grave one day and sang the song. Not McCormack perhaps. But with resonance and true understanding.   *BK*

THE OLD BOG ROAD

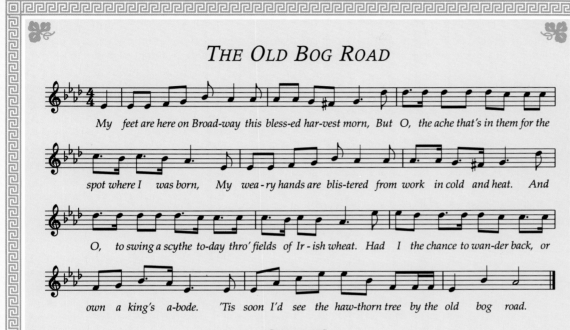

My feet are here on Broad-way this bless-ed har-vest morn, But O, the ache that's in them for the spot where I was born, My wea-ry hands are blis-tered from work in cold and heat. And O, to swing a scythe to-day thro' fields of Ir-ish wheat. Had I the chance to wan-der back, or own a king's a-bode. 'Tis soon I'd see the haw-thorn tree by the old bog road.

ABOVE: *Teresa Brayton from a photograph belonging to Ben Kiely*

2 My mother died last Springtide when Ireland's
    fields were green;
The neighbours said her waking was the finest
    ever seen.
There were snowdrops and primroses piled up beside
    her bed;
And Ferns Church was crowded when her funeral
    Mass was said,
But there was I on Broadway, with building bricks for
    load,
When they carried out her coffin from the old bog
    road.

3 When I was young and restless my mind was ill at
    ease,
Thro' dreaming of America and gold beyond the seas.
O, sorrow take their money, 'tis hard to get that same,
And what's the world to any man, where no one
    speaks his name?
I've had my day and here I am, with building
    bricks for load,
A long three thousand miles away from the old
    bog road.

4 There was a decent girl at home who used to walk
    with me;
Her eyes were soft and sorrowful, like sunbeams on
    the sea.
Her name was Mary Dwyer, but that was long
    ago,
And the ways of God are wiser than the things a
    man may know.
She died the year I left her, with building bricks
    for load,
I'd best forget the times we met on the old bog
    road.

5 Ah! life's a weary puzzle past finding out by man,
I take the day for what its worth and do the best I
    can,
Since no one cares a rush for me; what needs to
    make a moan.
I go my way, and draw my pay and smoke my pipe
    alone,
Each human heart must know its grief, tho' little
    be its load,
So God be with you Ireland, and the old bog road.

ABOVE: *'There were snowdrops and primroses piled up beside her bed ....'*

73

THE MOUNTAINS OF MOURNE

The Mountains of Mourne, though hardly mountains at all since no peak reaches 3,000 feet, are still a magnificent sight towering over Co. Down and the Irish Sea. They are well-loved by generations of Irish people, a landmark for sailors and a heart-felt memory for emigrants. The famous song was written by Percy French who described how the idea, words and music came together:

'Looking at the range of the Mourne Mountains from Skerries (on the east coast and some twenty miles from Dublin) one clear afternoon, I found myself repeating "The Mountains of Mourne sweep down to the sea". This line kept recurring to me till one day it wedded itself to an old Irish air, and the combination seemed so happy that I set to work, or rather shut myself up in my top room with pen, ink and paper, and waited. And so my most successful song, admirably arranged by Doctor Collison, was given to an applauding public'.

William Percy French was born on 1 May, 1854 in Cloonyquin, Co. Roscommon. He was of the Irish landed gentry, a son of 'the Big House', reared in luxury, educated at expensive English schools and eventually at Trinity College Dublin where he set a record as the student who took the longest time to gain a degree.

He did begin a career as an engineer in Ireland – he mockingly described himself as 'an Inspector of Drains' – and for a few short years he travelled the countryside mixing with small farmers and getting to know the lives of the ordinary people of Ireland. He relished every minute of these encounters with alert, nimble-witted humorous countrymen and women: but he was impatient with the details of his official occupation – he loved 'larking about' as he had done for years as an undergraduate – so he resigned in search of a better life. His family was no longer wealthy so he needed to earn a living.

Today, Percy French is well-remembered as the author of half-a-dozen celebrated songs that belong somewhere in the canon of Irish music in a genre all of their own, with titles like 'Phil the Fluter's Ball', 'Are Ye Right There, Michael?', and 'McBreen's Heifer'. He was also a fine painter, mainly of landscapes, and today his watercolours command high prices at auction. So, when he threw up his job in his mid-thirties, it was clear he was a man with many talents.

Nevertheless, the role in life he then chose for himself was a precarious one. He became an entertainer, travelling the country, spending his life on the road, appearing in parochial halls and music halls with a banjo and an easel, singing his songs, telling stories and doing lightning sketches. He was volatile, impulsive, untidy, careless, unbusiness-like and his greatest fault, according to his sister, was 'his disregard for his own and for his family's prosperity'.

There is no doubt that he thought of himself as a misfit – 'I was born a boy', he said, 'and I remain a boy'– but it would be more accurate to describe him as a student who remained a student. His songs are mischievous and irreverent, poking fun but never wounding. However, he was in tune with his times, with the people he lived among, and his songs conjure up the spirit of those times and people.

His songs were not intended to be part of Irish traditional music, though from time to time traditional music was a source of his tunes, just as he drew freely from colloquial speech for the best of his lyrics. And he made no attempt to copy from the stage-Irish scene either. Indeed he didn't need to copy anything for he was witty and sophisticated, a free-roving spirit whose work always turned out funny, a 'drop-out' who dropped out before the word was invented.   *DH*

ABOVE: *a detail from Sir Robert Ponsonby Staples sketch of Percy French*

BELOW: *the Mourne Mountains reach the sea at Newcastle, Co. Down.*

THE MOUNTAINS OF MOURNE

Oh Ma-ry this Lon-don's a won-der-ful sight, With the peo-ple here work-ing by day and by night, They don't sow po-ta-toes nor bar-ley nor wheat, But there's gangs of them dig-ging for gold in the street, At least when I asked them that's what I was told, so I just took a hand at this dig-ging for gold, But for all that I found there I might as well be, Where the Moun-tains of Mourne sweep down to the sea.

2 I believe that when writing a wish you expressed
As to how the fine ladies of London were dressed
Well if you believe me, when asked to a ball
They don't wear a top to their dresses at all
Oh, I've seen them myself, and you could not in truth
Say if they were bound for a ball or a bath.
Don't be starting them fashions now Mary Macree,
Where the mountains of Mourne sweep down to the sea.

3 You remember young Peter O'Loughlin of course –
Well, now he is here at the head of the Force.
I met him today, I was crossing the Strand,
And he stopped the whole street with one wave of his hand;
And there we stood talking of days that are gone,
While the whole population of London looked on;
But for all these great powers he's wishful like me,
To be back where dark Mourne sweeps down to the sea.

4 There's beautiful girls here – oh, never you mind
With beautiful shapes Nature never designed,
And lovely complexions, all roses and cream
But O'Loughlin remarked with regard to the same;
That if at those roses you venture to sip,
The colours might all come away on your lip;
So I'll wait for the wild rose that's waiting for me,
Where the mountains of Mourne sweep down to the sea.

ABOVE: snow dusts the Silent Valley in the Mourne Mountains.

BELOW: an old sheet music cover of Percy French's famous song

CARRICKFERGUS

ABOVE: the town of Carrickfergus, Co. Antrim, at sunset

This is an old song that has become newly popular and widely known mainly through the recordings of the singer Van Morrison and others. Carrickfergus stands on Belfast Lough about eleven miles from that city.

From Belfast, once you get off the motorway, it's a pleasant drive along the lough, leaving the smoke and chimneys behind.

The Fergus who gave the town its name – 'The Rock of Fergus' – is, according to an old story, Fergus MacErc, a local chieftain who became king of Scotland, a distinction that was ultimately his undoing insofar as he drowned, poor man, on one of his comings and goings between his two kingdoms.

It is a picturesque port in an old world setting. Nowadays the town's greatest attraction is Carrickfergus Castle. Even at first sight it is impressive in its massiveness, long and low and standing dramatically on a rock overlooking the harbour, commanding all shipping routes into and out of Belfast. Old cannons point through the battlements towards phantom fleets with billowing sails, and even towards the foreshore where nowadays children play on the sand.

It was built by one of the Anglo-Norman conquistadors in the twelfth century, shortly after their arrival in Ireland. It was one of the first of a series of castles built throughout Ireland by the invaders, to help secure their tenure in hostile territory. These strong castles, combined with their builders' talent for military organisation, enabled a handful of Anglo-Norman lords to rule half the country within a few decades of their arrival.

Carrickfergus Castle has lived through lively and dramatic times, numerous battles and burnings, before settling at last for a peaceful existence as a museum and as a pleasant place to contemplate the ebb and flow of centuries. Tableaux help to build the atmosphere. There is brave (let's be charitable and not say ruthless) John de Courcy, mounted and looking gallant with his white livery marked with red eagles, and his lady Affreca looking ever over the sea towards her home, the Isle of Man. Visitors with an active imagination can add to the mood by pretending that the chimney stack in the distance is the round tower of a Celtic church, which would have been likely in those times.

It is a popular tourist ploy to have oneself photographed with one – or all – of 'The Gallant Gunners of the Royal Artillery' who are frozen in the act of muzzle-loading one of the cannon.

In the eighteenth century a family named Jackson kept an inn near the town's North Gate. One of that family, born in South Carolina, went on to become President Andrew Jackson of the United States.

From Carrickfergus, it is a glorious drive northwards along the Antrim coast road, where great cliffs of black basalt contrast with bright chalk crags and gentle bays. The coast road opens to the Glens of Antrim, nine of them, each different in character, but all sharing the elemental beauty of woods and waterfalls. Until

CARRICKFERGUS

I wish I was_____ in Car - rick - fer - gus on - ly for
nights_____ in Bal - ly - grand I would swim o - ver_____ the deep - est
o - cean on - ly for nights_____ in Bal - ly - grand. Ah but the sea is
wide_____ and I can - not swim o - ver,_____ nor have I wings_____ so I could
fly I wish I could meet_____ a hand - some
boat - man_____ to fer - ry me o - ver_____ to my love and die.

2 *Now in Kilkenny it is reported*
They've marble stones there as black as ink
With Gold and Silver I would transport her.
But I'll sing no more now 'till I get a drink.
I'm drunk today, but then I'm seldom sober –
A handsome rover from town to town,
Ah! but I'm sick now my days are over,
Come all ye young lads and lay me down.

ABOVE: *Scottish pipes are often heard in Ireland at Irish dancing festivals.*

BELOW: *Carrickfergus Castle, a Norman fort that today is a museum*

the coast road was built in the 1830s, these glens were completely isolated and remote. Consequently old ways and customs were preserved there, and a great richness of Gaelic myth and legend.

Farther north the road leads on to the spectacular geological curiosity known as 'The Giant's Causeway', a rampart of rock columns leading like stepping stones down to and under the sea, as if to some subterranean city. It was, of course, built by the giant Finn MacCool.   *EH*

THE ROSE OF MOONCOIN

ABOVE: *River Suir, Co. Kilkenny. 'Flow on, lovely river, flow gently along ....'*

BELOW: *a nineteenth-century engraving of a departing emigrant ship*

I spent a morning of my youth in Mooncoin with a gloriously eccentric genius of a newspaper editor, a Quaker actor and, later in the golden evening, a Native American reporter, a man whose name in his own tongue was Whispering Wind. It was a long time ago, a day of the locally famous Piltown Agricultural Show, the world full of heavy red-flanked bullocks and Kilkenny fruit and flowers captured in little wooden competition crates. And scones and fruit cakes bursting with raisined and sultaned pride on the white tables of comparison.

You will not find Mooncoin in the glossy guidebooks. But this gentle small place, smocked with heavy greenery ruffled by breezes from the River Suir, is almost at the Waterford end of the beautiful road that falls down from Clonmel into Waterford. We went there because my globe-trotting editor, the magnificent Smokey Joe Walshe of *The Munster Express*, had met Whispering Wind at a World Fair earlier in the year in Canada. And Whispering Wind had been working for a newspaper in Moose Jaw in Saskatchewan, and one of the old hot-lead printers for his paper was a Wexford man who was a relation of Seamus Kavanagh, writer of 'The Rose of Mooncoin'. And because the printer, in his cups, sang the song so hauntingly in the saloons of Moose Jaw, the sensitive Native

American twisted his holiday route to get to Mooncoin and see the very place where the fisherman sported with his short boat and line on the breast of a river an emigrant never forgot.

Smokey Joe had met everybody in his lifetime. He told us, over our pints, that Seamus Kavanagh came from Wexford, around Taghmon, and had been 'a hardy man' who was a freedom fighter in the Easter Rising and the later events of the War of Independence.

Smokey had interviewed Kavanagh in Enniscorthy about twenty years earlier. Seamus Kavanagh had silvery hair, a low voice, deep-set eyes, a great love of rural Ireland, and, because he had a cold at the time of the interview, he had only been able to whisper the lines of the great songs he had written. Like 'The Rose of Mooncoin'. Like 'Moonlight in Mayo'. Like, surprisingly, from his early Dublin years, the saga of 'Biddy Mulligan', the street vendor who was the Queen of Dublin's colourful Coombe.

Smokey Joe had a powerful Jaguar car at a time when the rest of the Irish had only Fords. He had a turbo-charged intellect of equal force. That day, sliding along the narrow roads by the Suir so that Whispering Wind could see the beauty of south Kilkenny and Waterford, he used the phrase 'the Hidden Ireland' thirty years before it was fashionable. And the Quaker actor, one of that most gentle of peoples, sang 'The Rose of Mooncoin' as we went the way.

The hauntingly simple song, in which, like so many other emigrant songs, dear Molly sails away o'er the dark rolling foam from the gentle river, has, however, another life. It is the definitive Kilkenny song, especially it is Kilkenny's hurling anthem. When the perennial giants of Leinster hurling stride out on to the sporting fields of the Hidden Ireland, or into Croke Park itself, striped in black and amber jerseys and equipped with usually matchless silken skills, the bands always play 'The Rose of Mooncoin'. Flow on, flow on, flow on.

Mooncoin's own hurlers have always been a force in Kilkenny hurling. The little Suirside village may often be missed in the guidebooks but it is marked large on the hurling map of Ireland. Emigration of all the thousands of beautiful girls and young men has not robbed this greened corner of its local pride and power.

The song that mourns the forced departure of poor Molly today more often salutes the strength and force and life of 'Hidden Ireland'.

The Native American called Whispering Wind already knew the air and he wrote down the lyrics in shorthand as the Quaker sang them, there by the Suir, so long ago. And though there was no boat on the river that day the thrush and robin did entwine sweet notes. And there were sunbeams aplenty. Is there somebody today in Moose Jaw who can sing, 'The Rose of Mooncoin'? I bet there is.   *CMcC*

ABOVE: *a cottage in the little village of Mooncoin in Co. Kilkenny*

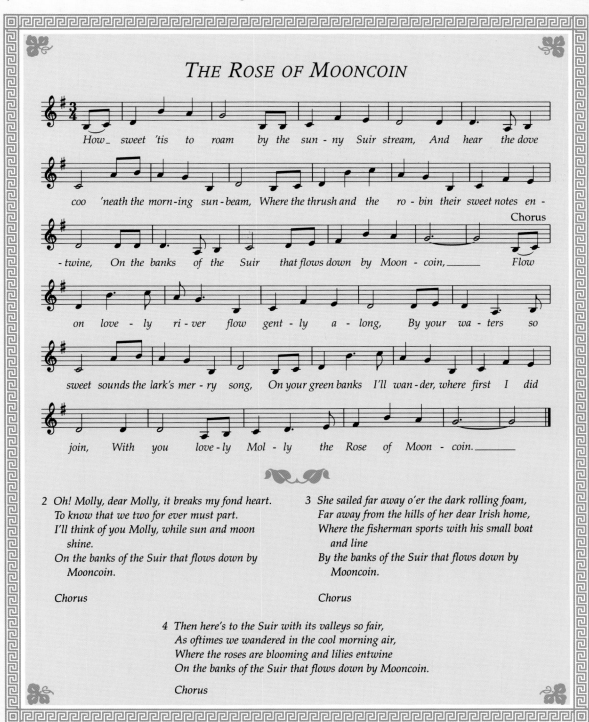

THE ROSE OF MOONCOIN

How sweet 'tis to roam by the sunny Suir stream, And hear the dove coo 'neath the morning sun-beam, Where the thrush and the robin their sweet notes en-twine, On the banks of the Suir that flows down by Moon-coin,____

Chorus

Flow on lovely river flow gently along, By your waters so sweet sounds the lark's merry song, On your green banks I'll wander, where first I did join, With you love-ly Mol-ly the Rose of Moon-coin.____

2 Oh! Molly, dear Molly, it breaks my fond heart.
To know that we two for ever must part.
I'll think of you Molly, while sun and moon shine.
On the banks of the Suir that flows down by Mooncoin.

Chorus

3 She sailed far away o'er the dark rolling foam,
Far away from the hills of her dear Irish home,
Where the fisherman sports with his small boat and line
By the banks of the Suir that flows down by Mooncoin.

Chorus

4 Then here's to the Suir with its valleys so fair,
As oftimes we wandered in the cool morning air,
Where the roses are blooming and lilies entwine
On the banks of the Suir that flows down by Mooncoin.

Chorus

ABOVE: *a Kilkenny hurler. 'The Rose of Mooncoin' is the Kilkenny hurling song.*

MÁIRE, MY GIRL

ABOVE: 'Over the dim blue hills rests my heart ever ....'

'Treason is put in a fascinating, tolerant and intelligent shape. Of course the Saxon comes in for it; but no Saxon could feel over-vexed at being railed at so eloquently in his own language.'

Those are the words of a decent, good-humoured critic writing in the *London Review* in 1869 about John Casey's second collection of poetry *The Rising of the Moon*. The *London Review* critic was very observant, for John Keegan Casey was a gentle romantic poet, but at the same time full of nationalist fervour which was reflected in his work. He was born in Mount Dalton not too far from Mullingar in Co. Westmeath in 1846. He was the son of a small

ABOVE: the monument to John Casey at Mount Dalton, his birthplace

MÁIRE, MY GIRL

O - ver the dim blue hills strays a wild ri - ver,

O - ver the dim blue hills rests my heart ev - er,

Dear - er and bright - er than jew - els and pearls,

Dwells she in beau - ty there, Mái - re my girl.

2 Down upon Claris heath shines the soft berry,
   On the brown harvest tree droops the red cherry.
   Sweeter thy honey lips, softer the curl,
   Straying adown thy cheeks, Máire, my girl.

3 'Twas on a April eve that I first met her;
   Many an eve shall pass ere I forget her.
   Since my young heart has been wrapped in a whirl,
   Thinking and dreaming of Máire, my girl.

4 She is too kind and fond ever to grieve me,
   She has too pure a heart e'er to deceive me.
   Were I Tyrconnell's chief or Desmond's earl,
   Life would be dark, wanting Máire, my girl.

5 Over the dim blue hills strays a wild river,
   Over the dim blue hills rests my heart ever.
   Fairer and dearer than jewel or pearl,
   Dwells she in beauty there, Máire, my girl.

farmer, but while very young took a great interest in literature, particularly poetry. When only sixteen-years old, his first poem appeared in the *Nation* under the pen name Leo, which he used throughout his short life. He got involved in the Fenian movement in the 1860s and was arrested and imprisoned in 1867. His health was never good and this experience would not have helped as he died from what seems to have been tuberculosis at the young age of twenty-four on St. Patrick's Day, 1870. They say that up to 50,000 people attended his funeral.

The lyrics of John Keegan Casey show a tenderness of heart and a deep attachment to his own countryside west of Mullingar and the River Inny, which he remembers with nostalgia:

> No more by Inny's bank I sit,
> Or rove the meadows brown,
> But count the weary hours away,
> Pent in this dismal town;
> I cannot breathe the pasture air,
> My father's homestead view,
> Or see another face like thine,
> My gentle Cailín Rua.

This is a part of Ireland which deserves to be better known and explored, from the big lakes of Owel, Ennell and Derravaragh over to the Inny River and westwards again into Longford and the countryside of another poet, Oliver Goldsmith.

'Máire, My Girl' is the best loved of 'Leo's' songs and was known in far away places and by lots of people who never heard of John Keegan Casey or the Inny River. It was recorded by many famous singers including John McCormack as far back as 1912, and the celebrated Austrian tenor of a generation ago, Richard Tauber.   *BK*

ABOVE: Mount Dalton estate, Co. Westmeath, in early springtime

LEFT: Lough Owel in the part of Westmeath beloved by the poet John Casey

81

SLÁN LE MÁIGH

Farewell to the Maigue

ABOVE: *a detail from J.G. Mulvany's nineteenth-century 'View of Kilmallock'*

BELOW: *sunset over the River Maigue near Adare in Co. Limerick, land of poets*

Coshma (*Cois Máighe*) is a barony in the middle of the County of Limerick, stretching from the Cork border near Ráth Luirc, and including Adare (often said to be the prettiest village in Ireland), Croom, and Bruff. Coshma means simply the lands along the River Maigue, although many important places on or near its banks and tributaries – Pallaskenry, Kilmallock, Bruree, for example – are in neighbouring baronies. The barony hardly counts as a unit now, of course, and the Coshma of the poets was more extensive than the Coshma of the maps. Any poet living near the river in the middle of the eighteenth century was thought qualified to be one of the poets of the Maigue, a court of poetry located in Croom 'of the Merriment'.

The name Coshma lives on mainly because of the poem 'Slán le Máigh' by Aindrias Mac Craith. Seán Ó Tuama 'of the Wit' and Aindrias are considered the chief poets of the Maigue

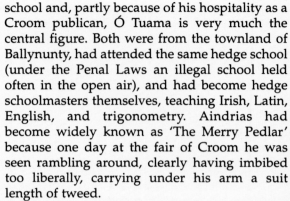

school and, partly because of his hospitality as a Croom publican, Ó Tuama is very much the central figure. Both were from the townland of Ballynunty, had attended the same hedge school (under the Penal Laws an illegal school held often in the open air), and had become hedge schoolmasters themselves, teaching Irish, Latin, English, and trigonometry. Aindrias had become widely known as 'The Merry Pedlar' because one day at the fair of Croom he was seen rambling around, clearly having imbibed too liberally, carrying under his arm a suit length of tweed.

Love is one of the main themes of the Pedlar's poems, and this marks him out from his fellow Maigue poets. He was judged to be something of a womaniser by a new parish priest of Croom and he was banished. Settling down in the village of Ballyneety about nine miles away, he found that his reputation had preceded him. The women in particular gave him the cold shoulder. Although only that short distance from Croom, his song in praise of Coshma is often classified as one of exile in school anthologies because of its strong note of loss and longing. Some years later the next parish priest of Croom turned out to be a friend and fellow-poet and the Merry Pedlar was allowed to return home.

Ó Tuama died in 1775 and is buried in Croom. Mac Craith lived on for another twenty years, residing for the most part in his native Ballynunty. He is buried in Kilmallock.

A convincing case can be made for the claim that the limerick was invented by the two poets, when Ó Tuama wrote verses in praise of himself as publican. This is James Clarence Mangan's version of a verse from Mac Craith's reply:

> 0'Toomey! You boast yourself handy
> At setting good ale and bright brandy,
> But the fact is your liquor
> Makes everyone sicker
> I tell you that, I, your friend Andy.

'Slán le Máigh' is usually sung to the same air as 'The Bells of Shandon' and, although it is thought not an entirely suitable match, the song continues to be a favourite with choirs.   *DB*

SLÁN LE MÁIGH

O Slán is céad ón dtaobh seo ua-im Cois Máigh na gcaor na gcraobh, na gcruach. Na stát na séad, na saor, na slua, Na ndán, na ndreacht, na dtrean gan ghruaim. Och, och, och ón is breoi-te mi-se gan chuid, gan chó-ir, gan chóip, gan chiste, gan sult, gan seod, gan spórt, gan spionn-adh, ó seol-adh mé chun ua-ig-nis.

ABOVE: a nineteenth-century engraving of a wandering poet

BELOW: Aindrias Mac Craith's gravestone at Kilmallock, Co. Limerick

Slán go héag dá saorfhir suairc,
Dá dáimh da héigs da cléir dá suadha,
Dom' chairde cléibh gan chlaon gan chluain
Gan cháim gan chaon gan chraos gan chruas.

Slán dá n-éis da béithibh uaim –
Dá gcáil dá gcéill da scéimh dá snua –
Dá mná go léir, dá gcéim dá gcuaird,
Dá bpráisc dá bplé dá méinn dá mbua.

Slán thar aon don té ná luaim,
'Si an bhánchnis bhéasach bhéaltais bhuach,
Chuir tráth chun sléibhe mé i gcéin im' ruaig –
'Sí grá mo chléibh 'bé in Eirinn cuach.

1 One hundred and one farewells I send from this
    place
  To Coshma of the berries, the boughs, the
    abundance
  The farms the properties, the craftsmen, the
    crowds,
  The poems, the stories and the cheerful heroes.

2 Alas, my grief! I am in anguish,
  With no belongings or supplies, company or money,
  Without any enjoyments, valuables, or diversions
  Since I was driven to this place of loneliness.

3 Farewell till death to its pleasant freemen,
  To its artistic company, its poets, its clergy, its
    litterati,
  To my bosom friends free from deceit and flattery,
  Faultless and without subterfuge, greed, or
    stinginess.

4 After them, fond farewell to its maidens,
  Their reputation, their intelligence, beauty and
    complexion,
  To all its women with their dignity and busy ways,
  Their teasing tricks, their conversation, good nature
    and gifts.

5 And farewell beyond all others to one who will be
    nameless,
  The lady-like, soft-lipped, joyous fair one,
  Who banished me once to a life of wandering.
  The love of my heart, but for Ireland I'll not tell
    her name.

ÚNA BHÁN

As you travel northwestward from Athlone to Roscommon through Castlerea to Boyle there is a perceptible change of light, of expanding sky and a sense of the presence of water with the Shannon and Lough Ree to the east, the River Suck to the west and many lakes.

To the north the River Boyle flows into the lovely Lough Key which lies above the historic Moylurg or Plains of Boyle celebrated in what Frank O'Connor and David Greene have called 'one of the most brilliant poems in Irish' written in the tenth century and reflecting the distinct quality of the district in winter – 'Wide Moylurg is cold tonight, the snow is higher than the hill, the deer cannot reach their food … the storm has spread over everything … every downhill channel is a river and every ford a flooded lake'.

Here too at Rathcroghan is the starting point of the heroic old Irish epic story *Táin Bó Cuailgne* (The Cattle Raid of Cooley). 'Once upon a time it befell Ailill and Maeve that, when their royal bed had been prepared for them in Rathcroghan in Connacht, they spoke together as they lay on their pillow …' A storied land.

Castle Island on Lough Key was for centuries a seat of the Mac Dermotts, a member of which family was the eponymous *Úna Bhán* (Fair Una) and because of this the passionate and elaborately wrought love song is romantically, but inaccurately, associated with Lough Key. Its actual location is somewhat further south close to the village of Ballymoe.

Douglas Hyde wrote: 'I do not think there is any

song more widely spread throughout the country and more common in the mouth of the people than the poem which strong Thomas Costello … composed over the unfortunate and handsome girl Una Mac Dermott to whom he had given love'.

The story of the frustrated love of Thomas Costello and Una Mac Dermott was rooted in the political and social exigencies of the mid-seventeenth century: their families had taken opposing sides and Costello had lost out as a result of the Cromwellian Settlement. But the passionately tormented love song said to have been composed by Thomas Costello survived, and passed with its accompanying folklore into the folk repertoire. The tradition tells how Thomas fell in love with Úna, whose family refused to consent to their marriage. Úna was stricken with love sickness and Thomas was allowed to visit her, but although she responded to his presence, consent was still withheld, and Thomas left, swearing not to return if he was not recalled before crossing the river to his own home. He lingered at the ford, but eventually crossed just as word came – too late. Úna died of a broken heart and was buried on an island on Lough Key. Thomas used to swim his horse to the island every night to lament their lost love, and when he was found dead at her island burial-place he was buried in the same graveyard close

ABOVE RIGHT: a detail from 'The Pride of the Village' by Edward Sheil: the love-sick Una?

BELOW: Mac Dermott's Castle on an islet in Lough Key, Co. Roscommon

ÚNA BHÁN

O Ún - a Bhá - n, you were____ all____ I had_____ eyes for; Your death was caused by a false____ ad - viser_____ I wish to the_____ Lord_____ I was warned____ to be wis - er, And to wait by__ the wa - - ter, till you called me_____ be - side you.

2 O Úna Bhán, like a rose on a garden wall,
  Like a golden bowl in a noble banquet hall,
  Sweet music you composed on the road going
    grand and tall
  And my grief I never owned you or held you in
    my arms at all.

3 O Úna Bhán, it was you who drove me mad;
  O Úna, 'twas you and your beauty tore me from
    God;
  O Úna, I was ruined by the view of your fine fair
    head,
  And if I could choose, I'd sooner be blind or dead.

ABOVE: 'Two ash trees grew from the graves and entwined over them.'

beside her. Two ash trees grew from the graves, and entwined over them.

It was Douglas Hyde, who grew up at Frenchpark where he learned Irish and came to love the songs and stories of the people, who popularised in English the song and story of 'Úna Bhán' in his *Love Songs of Connacht* (1893), a book which Yeats described as 'the coming of a new power into literature' and which profoundly influenced Lady Gregory and John Millington Synge.

The song now usually consists of four or five verses but the oldest manuscript version contains forty-five verses which were transcribed around the year 1772 by Brian Ó Fearghail from the parish of St. John on the banks of Lough Ree; he lived most of his life at Ballymoe close to where the events of the song and story took place. It is quite likely that he wrote down the song for Charles O'Conor (1710-90) the well-known Irish scholar and historian who lived at Bellanagare, a short distance from Douglas Hyde's birthplace, and who was closely associated with the foundation of the Royal Irish Academy in 1785 where this manuscript is now preserved. *EÓhA*

THE MUSKERRY SPORTSMAN

'Ye maids of Duhallow ... ' Where is Duhallow and, for that matter, where is Muskerry? They are neither parishes, villages, or postal towns, and gazetteers or guides are of little help in finding out their location or extent. They were in fact ancient petty kingdoms, divisions of Desmond or South Munster, and later they became baronies. 'Wide Duhallow', as one poet named it, stretched over into the Sliabh Luachra country of Kerry. Ballydesmond, or Kingwilliamstown as it was up to forty years ago, is part of the barony.

The baronies gave the status of capitals to Kanturk and Macroom. And one event in Duhallow had almost county standing: the annual sports in Banteer. Ever since Kickham's novel, *Knocknagow* (1879), and long before the Olympic movement, young men all over Munster were anxious to emulate the athletic feats of Matt the Thrasher 'for the credit of the little village'. And they did indeed do that, as the records of the Olympics show. Duhallow reached its peak when Kanturk man Dr. Pat O'Callaghan won gold medals in 1928 and 1932.

Railways were in their heyday in Ireland, and particularly in Cork, in the 1890s. This helped in the codification of games and in the creation of a competitive spirit in athletics. One could travel directly to Banteer by rail from Dungarvan, or Dingle, or Valentia, but not from Macroom. If Thady's 'carriage' came by rail over the hills of

ABOVE: *hurling sticks for all the family outside a shop in Macroom, Co. Cork*

BELOW: *hurling in progress: the making of another 'Bould Thady Quill'?*

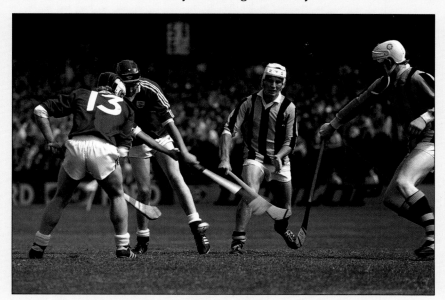

Kilcorney it must have been, with some generous poetic license, from Millstreet Station. But it is more likely that a man of his stature came in a horse-drawn conveyance.

One hundred years after he had thrilled the maids of Duhallow, Thady would be delighted with such idle speculation about the details of travel. The simple truth is, alas, that he was never any kind of athlete. The story goes that he was employed by a Muskerry farmer, one Johnny Tom Gleeson in Ballinagree, a townland north of Macroom, and that, as the great euphemism has it, he never killed himself working. Driving a cow to the fair of Macroom was all right but, being given to day-dreaming perhaps, he was unable to address himself to the more rigorous of farming chores. And one suspects that his master may not have been a model farmer. He had the reputation of being a good ballad maker. Excellence of achievement in such disparate occupations is rare.

Johnny Tom took it into his head to pen a satirical verse about Thady and, as Thady did not understand satire, the result was totally unexpected. For a full month he worked hard, so pleased was he with his new fame as an athlete. And, so, month by month, Johnny Tom made new verses, every verse discovering a fresh virtue or skill: Thady the huntsman, Thady's attraction for women, Thady the hurler, Thady the patriot and Parnellite, Thady the pugilist .... Although it is said that he got a year's work out of Thady in this manner, most songbooks give a few verses only. But singers often add a verse or two, to cover events of a date later than Parnell's death, or to forecast a drubbing for Tipperary in the next Munster hurling final. The Duhallow and Muskerry countryside along the Kerry border is justly famous for its balladmakers. Many of them, in places such as Kilgarvan, Rathmore, Ballingeary, were Irish speakers and had inherited a rich tradition of versifying. 'The Bould Thady Quill' was given national currency when Walton's Musical Instrument Galleries included it in one of their songbooks almost fifty years ago. The air was well known, having been previously wedded to that other great song celebrating the spirit of place, Raftery's 'Killeadan', which was already established in the schools' repertoire. And, of course, that great rollicking chorus also helped.   DB

THE MUSKERRY SPORTSMAN

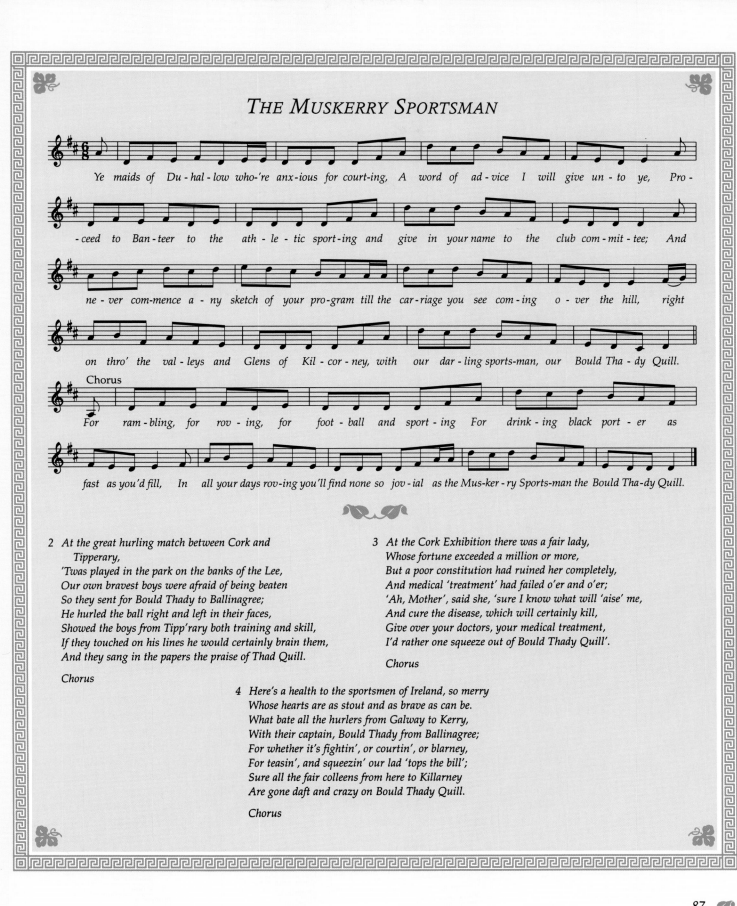

Ye maids of Du - hal - low who're anx - ious for court - ing, A word of ad - vice I will give un - to ye, Pro -

-ceed to Ban - teer to the ath - le - tic sport - ing and give in your name to the club com - mit - tee; And

ne - ver com - mence a - ny sketch of your pro - gram till the car - riage you see com - ing o - ver the hill, right

on thro' the val - leys and Glens of Kil - cor - ney, with our dar - ling sports - man, our Bould Tha - dy Quill.

Chorus

For ram - bling, for rov - ing, for foot - ball and sport - ing For drink - ing black port - er as

fast as you'd fill, In all your days rov - ing you'll find none so jov - ial as the Mus - ker - ry Sports - man the Bould Tha - dy Quill.

2 At the great hurling match between Cork and
    Tipperary,
'Twas played in the park on the banks of the Lee,
Our own bravest boys were afraid of being beaten
So they sent for Bould Thady to Ballinagree;
He hurled the ball right and left in their faces,
Showed the boys from Tipp'rary both training and skill,
If they touched on his lines he would certainly brain them,
And they sang in the papers the praise of Thad Quill.

Chorus

3 At the Cork Exhibition there was a fair lady,
Whose fortune exceeded a million or more,
But a poor constitution had ruined her completely,
And medical 'treatment' had failed o'er and o'er;
'Ah, Mother', said she, 'sure I know what will 'aise' me,
And cure the disease, which will certainly kill,
Give over your doctors, your medical treatment,
I'd rather one squeeze out of Bould Thady Quill'.

Chorus

4 Here's a health to the sportsmen of Ireland, so merry
Whose hearts are as stout and as brave as can be.
What bate all the hurlers from Galway to Kerry,
With their captain, Bould Thady from Ballinagree;
For whether it's fightin', or courtin', or blarney,
For teasin', and squeezin' our lad 'tops the bill';
Sure all the fair colleens from here to Killarney
Are gone daft and crazy on Bould Thady Quill.

Chorus

SPANCIL HILL

ABOVE: horses and horsemen congregate at Spancilhill Fair each June.

BELOW: Robbie McMahon at home in Spancilhill in June 1995

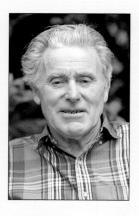

The chapels of the Midlands are different. There are no mountains here to press against the stained-glass windows or to hinder the eternal horizons above and about. And it was in the Midlands chapel of Portarlington that Brendan McMahon from Spancilhill in the County Clare was Requiem Massed last year after dying before his time. The skies were white and empty with the infinity of space and grief.

The family asked Brendan's famous brother Robbie to sing one song at the Requiem Mass. The song was the ballad that Robbie, above any other balladeer, has made famous over the past forty-five years or more. Robbie sang it maybe better than he ever sang it in his life, this ballad of life and longing and losing, all the eleven verses of the original version, and there were more tears in Portarlington that morning than in all the rest of Ireland.

Sometimes a ballad becomes a hymn. It is that way with 'Spancil Hill', not just that day in Portarlington, but anywhere today where people from the County Clare are flung together far away from home. The song talks of the emigrant awaking in California, many miles from Spancilhill. But it could be any crossroads in Clare, not just that famous one east of Ennis, and California can be anywhere on earth.

But it was from California, says Robbie McMahon, that the song came back to Spancilhill around the turn of the century. It was written there by Michael Considine, who emigrated from Spancilhill to the United States in 1870 at the age of twenty. Considine was highly intelligent, articulate, and somewhat delicate of health too. He went first to Boston but, later, probably because of the healthier climate, to California. Here he studied hard and worked hard, eventually qualifying as an accountant. However, all his life, he never forgot the green townlands around the Cross of Spancilhill, where the great week-long fair was held every June, filling the narrow roads with excitement and rural commerce. Sensing his approaching death, because of ill health, Considine wrote his ode to home and its people and sent it back home to his nephew John Considine. He died not long afterwards.

We must jump a few decades to a time, nearly a half-century ago, when Robbie, himself only a boy, was in the Considine household. He was interested in singing even then – with a voice like a bell – and the words were given to him by Maria Keehan of the Considine family. He learned them and the air that went with them.

A little later Robbie was again in one of the Considine houses. It was a night for celebration because the family had purchased a Tilley lamp and, better still, had managed to get the relatively complicated apparatus to work. Relatively complicated? The Tilley lamps required the skills of a magician to get them working properly. After much effort, on this night the white light flooded the house with joy. A song was called for and Robbie was commanded to sing. The man of the house, stern of face and with a hat on his head, sat in the corner listening intently. The song was a kind of family heirloom, not to be trifled with. At last, says Robbie, he saw the man visibly relax, after five or six verses, and leaned back and allowed his hat to slide over his closed eyes. It was good, and he told Robbie so immediately afterwards.

Times change. The fair of Spancilhill, though it has shrunk from its traditional week to just one jam-packed June day of horses and horsey men, still survives and survives stoutly. The last of the tailor Quigley's daughters only died a few years ago in Ennis. Though he has sung the song that has become 'his' now all over the world, Robbie

SPANCIL HILL

Last night as I lay dream-ing of plea-sant days gone by___ Me

mind been bent on ram-bling to Ire-land I___ did fly,___ I

stepped a-board a vi-sion and follow-ed with_ a will,___ till___

next I came to an-chor at the cross_ near Span-cil Hill.___

2 *Enchanted by the novelty, delighted with the scene,*
Where in my early boyhood I oftentimes had been,
I thought I heard a murmur, I think I hear it still,
'Tis the little stream of water at the cross of Spancil Hill.

3 *It being the twenty-third of June, the day before the fair,*
Sure Erin's sons and daughters, they all assembled there;
The young, the old, the stout and the bold, came there for sport and kill,
What a curious combination at the fair of Spancil Hill.

4 *I paid a flying visit to my first and only love,*
She's as pure as any lily and as gentle as a dove.
She threw her arms around me, saying 'Mike, I love you still!'
She's Mac the Ranger's daughter, the pride of Spancil Hill.

5 *I thought I'd stoop and kiss her as I did in the days of yore,*
Says she 'Mike, you're only joking, as you often were before.'
The cock flew on the roost again, he crew both loud and shrill,
And I woke up in California, far far from Spancil Hill.

ABOVE: *California dreaming, 'far, far from Spancil Hill ….'*

BELOW: *a colourful mural on a pub wall in Spancilhill, Co. Clare*

McMahon still lives and sings in Spancilhill. He will be singing there, God willing, each June for many years to come when the old fair brings all its life to the quiet crossroads, filling Brohan's and Duggan's pubs with horse traders, tourists and singers who know the first verse, at least, of one of Ireland most popular ballads.

It is a song that will last maybe even longer than the famous horse fair it commemorates. It is a ballad to make men, even those with stern faces, lean back and relax. Brightly it burns, illuminating a time and a crossroads and a people, golden bright as a Tilley lamp.   CMcM

SLIABH NA mBAN

Slievenamon

The storied landmark of Slievenamon (in Gaelic, *Sliabh na mBan*: 'The mountain of the women') a mountain of old red sandstone, 2,368 feet high, dominates the great plain of south Tipperary where that county borders Kilkenny and Waterford. The name derives from the fairy women of Feimheann (pronounced Fevin), an ancient territorial name. Early Irish literature tells how the legendary warrior Finn Mac Cumhaill and his companions of the Fianna were enchanted there by the women of the mythological Tuatha Dé Danann, while the fairy mound on its slope is one of those locations where Finn is said to have gained mystic knowledge and access to the supernatural world to which Sliabh na mBan gave entry.

FAR RIGHT: Slievenamon from the Comeragh Mountains, Co. Tipperary

BELOW: the romantic mountain of Slievenamon at the close of the day

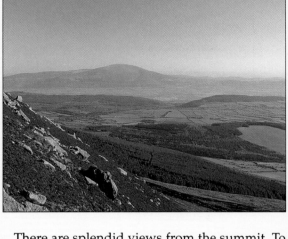

There are splendid views from the summit. To the north-west across an expansive chequer-work of bright green fields and darker woodlands lies that other historic eminence, the Rock of Cashel, while closer around its western shoulder flows the Anner. Southwards across the valley of the Suir to the Comeragh Mountains lies fertile farmland, wooded and well stocked. The telling remark 'This is indeed a land worth fighting for' is attributed to Oliver Cromwell while on his way to a serious rebuff at the Siege of Clonmel in 1650.

The brooding presence and ever-changing appearance of the mountain, which indeed gathers to itself 'all the coloured days', is reflected in the observations of Amhlaoibh Ó Súilleabháin (1780-1838), merchant, school-teacher, and antiquarian of Callan in Co. Kilkenny who kept a journal in Irish during the years 1827-35. 'Sliabh na mBan to the southwest is a beautiful sight under a cap of fog ... Sliabh na mBan was hidden in heavy black clouds like a dark oak wood ... Sliabh na mBan most glorious at sunset and beyond that the Galtees'. And the bitter political conflicts and triumphs of those years are recorded, 'There are thousands of bonfires on the hills of Ireland all around as far as I can see – on Sliabh na mBan and on every hill and mountain in the four counties'.

At the height of the Great Famine the mountain was a natural rallying point for the would-be revolutionary Young Irelanders. A crowd estimated at 50,000 gathered there in July

1848 to protest at the dire condition of the country, with thousands dying while a rich harvest ripened all around.

Fifty years before, the song 'Sliabh na mBan' (Slievenamon) lamented defeat in a local engagement in the rebellion of 1798. While the words are plangent with indignation at betrayal and regret for a lost opportunity, the defiantly soaring air and the insistent evocation of the sunlit slopes of Sliabh na mBan transcend the sense of loss. *EÓhA*

SLIABH NA MBAN

Oh bit-ter pain it is, that thus the day went A-gainst the Gael in that dread-ful fight, For how the stran - gers__ are mak - ing game of us, Our pikes are vain, they say, a-gainst their__ might, Our ma - jor came not, when dawn-ed that day on us, And we our-selves were is dis - or - der thrown, Like scat-tered herds we were with-out their__ dro - ver, On the sun - ny hill slopes of Slieve - na - mon.

2 Oh woe is me! those who fought so vainly,
   Who did not wait for the gath'ring then,
   Till from the Deisi*, and from western Eirinn
   Were heard the tramp of their mustered men.
   But yet I tell them, though sore befell them,
   That we'll keep their mem'ry with pike and spear,
   When we meet the yeomen, our bitter foemen,
   On Slievenamon ere another year.

3 Oh many the aged man, and youthful hero,
   That has been taken since that bitter time.
   In fetters bound lie they on the ground there,
   In dungeons dark, though unknown their crime.
   Their guards surround them, but we'll confound them.
   We'll strike them down and we'll hound them on,
   And our friends we'll free them, and soon release them,
   When days of peace dawn on Slievenamon.

4 The French, they say, are all in the bay now,
   With tall masts tap'ring on each gallant ship.
   They'll make a stay now in our green Eirinn,
   For that's the tale I hear, on ev'ry lip.
   If true that tale is, 'tis blessed this day I am,
   My heart like blackbird the thorn upon,
   When the trumpet's sounding, and swift steeds bounding,
   Upon the slopes of old Slievenamon.

*Deisi: pr. Day-sha, the district covered by west Waterford.

ABOVE: *prison conditions in Ireland in the nineteenth century: as the song claims, prisoners were indeed 'In fetters bound ... In dungeons dark ....'*

ACKNOWLEDGEMENTS

The Slide File, Dublin
pages: 5, 7, 13 both, 14 both, 15 bottom, 16 both, 19 top, 20 bottom, 23 top, 26 top, 27, 30 top, 31 top and bottom, 32 bottom, 34 both, 36 bottom, 37 both, 40 top and bottom left, 42 bottom, 45 both, 46 centre, 52 top, 54 bottom, 62 bottom, 66 left, 69 bottom, 74 bottom, 76, 77 bottom, 78 top, 81 bottom, 82 bottom, 84 bottom, 86 bottom and facing page.
Michael Diggin Photography, Tralee
pages: 12, 10, 11 both bottom, 17 both, 18 bottom, 24 top, 28 top left and bottom, 32 top, 38 both, 39 both, 40 bottom right, 41 top, 44 bottom, 47 bottom, 50, 51 bottom, 52 bottom, 53 top, 54 top, 55, 56 bottom, 57 bottom, 58, 63 bottom, 64 bottom, 77 top and 79 both, 80 both, 83 bottom, 85, 86 top, 88 both, 89 bottom and 90 both.
Bord Fáilte/Irish Tourist Board, Dublin
pages: 42 top right, courtesy of Tom Kelly, 51 top, courtesy of Michael Harkin, and 70 bottom, courtesy of the Earl of Meath and Brian Lynch.
Don Sutton International Photo Library, Dublin
pages: 6-7, 11 top, 15 top, 20 top right, 22 top, 24 bottom, 25, 42 top left, 46 top right and bottom, 56 top right, 57 top, 61, 63 top, 64 top, 68, 70 top, 73 bottom, 81 top and 89 top.
National Gallery of Ireland, Dublin
pages: 30 bottom, 35 top and 82 top
The Ulster Museum, Belfast
pages: 26 bottom and 74 top, both reproduced by permission of Mrs H. Radclyffe Dolling, 60 bottom, 66 bottom, reproduced by permission of Ms J. Donnelly.

Cork City Gaol, Cork
page 59 top
Cork Public Museum
page 59 bottom
The Gorry Gallery, Dublin
pages: 18 top, 23 bottom, 28 top right, 35 bottom, 36 top, reproduced by permission of Ms A. Yeats and Mr M. Yeats, 72 and 84 top.
The Royal Dragoon Guards, York
page 33
Ulster Folk and Transport Museum, Cultra
pages: 47 top, and 67, reproduced by permission of Ms E. I. Vitty.
The Percy French Society, Bangor, and Alan Tongue
pages: 20 top left and 75 bottom
Peters, Frazer & Dunlop Group, London, for permission to reprint the Frank O'Connor translation of Kilcash on page 65
The trustees of the Estate of Patrick Kavanagh, c/o Peter Fallon, Literary Agent, Loughcrew, Oldcastle, Co. Meath for permission to reprint Patrick Kavanagh's poem 'Raglan Road'
Mr D. Sealy for permission to reprint Douglas Hyde's translation of 'Contae Mhuigheo'

The publishers have used their best efforts to trace all copyright holders. They will, however, make the usual and appropriate arrangements with any who may have inadvertently been overlooked and who contact them.